Creating Your Life
as a Blessing

Jan. 19, 2015

Dear Zhanna,
So happy we met.
Enjoy my book! May

Creating Your Life
as a Blessing

Forty-one Personal Stories
with Lessons and Questions
to Guide You

God bless you always with
good health, a peaceful
heart, prosperity, and
your dreams coming true.

Carol Joy Goldstein-Hall

♡ Carol (858) 44-29085
carol joyand c@yahoo.com
www.technologiesfor
creating.com

Cover and inside author photos by Barbara Maynord.
Photographs of artwork by Nathan Stinson.
Illustrations by Sean Smith.
Back cover author photo by Stan Lawrence.

This book was printed in the United States of America.

To order additional copies of this book, contact:
Xlibris Corporation
1-888-795-4274
www.Xlibris.com
Orders@Xlibris.com
15446

Dedication

To my mother, Laura

A grateful thank you to my mother for her unending love, and her constant enthusiasm and support for my completing and publishing this book. Although my mother passed away in 1999, she will always have a special place in my heart.

To my beloved late husband, Glen

A heartfelt thank you for his deep love, patience, nurturing and incredible faith in God. He was a wonderful teacher and a blessing in my life.

To my two children, Nancy and Drew

Thank you for the difference you have made in my life, and for your special friendship, love, and support which I will cherish forever.

Contents

Acknowledgements

I would especially like to thank my late husband, Glen, for his years of patience and support. He has instilled me with a deeper love of the Lord, and trust in Him. I believe this has led me to follow my instincts and write this book.

Secondly, I owe a debt of gratitude for the brilliant mentoring and words of encouragement from Robert Fritz, author of *The Path of Least Resistance* and *Creating,* and founder of Technologies for Creating.® I'm also grateful to his wife, Rosalind, an excellent teacher of Structural Consulting, invented by Robert Fritz.

I would like to thank my parents for instilling in me my authentic desire to help people, my love of life, and my love and respect for God. In addition, I am grateful for their encouraging me to continue my piano studies, and for their providing me with many artistic and educational opportunities.

One of the most important things an author needs, especially if it is their first book, is a supportive, inspiring coach and editor. Thanks to Jenice Gharib, I was fortunate to receive her constant support and her excellent constructive feedback. Confidence in myself and my writing followed.

For her excellent skill at editing, typing and retyping of my many drafts of this book, I profusely thank my administrative assistant and friend, Jennifer Bennett. I am also grateful for her unending patience and perseverance.

Further gratitude is owed to John-Raphael Staude for his excellent coaching support. He helped me to think in a far more creative way, and he especially made me realize that I needed to be clear about the theme and structure for my book.

Lastly, I would like to acknowledge hundreds of my students who participated in my *Technologies for Creating®* courses as well as those who were my private clients. Thank you for being willing to stretch and commit yourselves to taking actions toward your deepest aspirations.

Author's Note

I have been teaching the Technologies for Creating® courses since 1984, and through teaching, consulting and speaking, I have seen literally hundreds of people's lives transformed. Writing this book is one way I believe I can touch many more lives.

My true commitment is to support people in living a life of freedom: the freedom to be themselves, as well as the freedom to create what they truly want. Many people have no idea they can really have this kind of life. Instead, they often stop asking themselves what they want because of prior disappointments, criticisms, fears, or lack of knowledge. They put their dreams on the back burner, or remain vague about them. Soon they become victims of their circumstances.

I have consulted with a wide range of people of all ages, from financially successful professionals, to teenagers, to men and women who have lost their jobs or marriages, to an eighty-nine year old woman who said she needed consulting so she could be true to herself. She wanted to take some art courses, but at the same time she did not want her time away to be detrimental to her elderly husband. (He was in a wheelchair and she loved him dearly.) Fortunately, she was able to follow her passion and accomplish her goal.

My commitment has been to help people realize that they do

have a choice in their lives. Several years ago, I worked with a young mother of two. She believed that no one would want her because she had a terminal illness. After she learned the creating principles, she made choices that led her to meeting a wonderful man who later became her husband. They moved into a beautiful home, and in a short period of time, her health was restored. We really don't know what's possible in our lives.

T.I.M.E.
Time is Marvelously Eternal

So many desires,
Be an artist or a dancer
What choice do you have?
Just pray for an answer.

Many hours in the day
I wonder where they go?
They pass away in seconds
Before we even know.

As I type this poem,
My grandfather clock strikes six,
I long to make a painting,
But the clock just ticks and ticks.

Then the telephone rings
And my good friend has to talk,
I need to say goodbye
And take my daily walk.

But my helpful, loving nature
Lets him cry on my shoulder,
Then my friend on the other end
Thanks me over and over.

Time is a funny thing,
We wish it would last and last.
And when we love what we're doing
We forget the painful past.

So stop complaining now
And decide what lights your fire.
Then make a lifetime vow
To spend time the way you desire.

Introduction

Look to this day
for it is life
the very life of life
In its brief course lie all
the realities and truths of existence
the joy of growth
the splendor of action
the glory of power
For yesterday is but a memory
And tomorrow is only a vision
But today well lived makes every yesterday
a memory of happiness
and every tomorrow a vision of hope
Look well, therefore, to this day.

—Ancient Sanskrit Poem

Most of us have seen or heard the last half of this poem, but have we been able to incorporate this philosophy into our lives? This is much easier said than done.

If we are hurt, disappointed, or treated unfairly, we often hold onto this pain. When we are worried or fearful about our future, we tend to be afraid to try new things, or we settle for what we think we can have.

What is so difficult about living our lives in the present moment? Perhaps we don't trust that our future will happen the way we desire. We lack faith.[1] We think we have to be the "Lone Ranger" and do it all by ourselves. Most of us have been taught a limited way of thinking such as, "You can't have your cake and eat it too," or "Cut your dreams down to reality." After numerous disappointments, people do what they can to avoid future pain. They may even give up their dreams entirely. Some people convince themselves that everything is just fine, even when it is not.

When I mention God throughout my book, please interpret God in your own personal way (i.e., Divine Spirit, Holy Spirit, higher power, the Lord, Christ, etc.). I do not mean to exclude any particular faith. These stories come from my own personal experiences. They were written for those of you who want to deepen your spiritual life, no matter what your spiritual tradition. As your faith deepens, your joy will increase, and you will experience many more of life's blessings moment to moment.

We all imagine blessings as a positive thing. *The American Heritage Dictionary* describes blessing as "a special favor granted by God." I have always felt that my children were a blessing from God. In spite of all the challenges that come along with being a mother, I would never have traded the experience.

The dictionary also describes blessing as "anything contributing to happiness, well-being or prosperity." In this light, we think of good things happening such as financial success, being in love, having good health, spending quality time with loved ones, and the blessings of life, liberty and the pursuit of happiness.

My Journey Towards Faith

Overall, I have had a joyful outlook on life and have tried to find the best in every situation. One of the reasons for this is because my mother, as much as she worried, still looked on the bright side of things. If something upsetting happened she would always chime in, "Remember, Carol, it could always be worse!"

In spite of my joyful attitude, as well as my belief in God, it has taken me many years and several workshops to let things flow and allow God to guide me. In other words, I had never learned what it meant to have true faith. Instead, I lived my life trying to control events and people, fearful that others might not like me. I was afraid that bad things might happen, so rather than enjoying the present moment, I worried a lot. The results were often disastrous. I felt like a victim, blaming other people when things didn't go my way. I didn't know what it was like to experience inner peace or the joy of being the person God created me to be. I was living life as a burden and didn't even know it. I wasn't aware I had a choice.

One day I realized that I wasn't living my life according to my values, especially the values of honesty and freedom. I gained the skills and confidence to create the life I truly desired after taking and then teaching Technologies for Creating®. This is a course about learning to create what truly matters to you, beyond what you think possible. Through many trials and tribulations described in the stories throughout this book, I was able to deepen my spiritual life, and start living from faith, rather than fear and worry.

Prior to my forty-seventh birthday, I had no idea that the Bible, thousands of years old, taught people how to live their lives as a blessing. I could never relate to the wording or the ideas. It always seemed like drudgery just to get through a few lines. When I was in my early twenties I signed up for a Bible study class and studied the book of Genesis with a rabbi. It felt like we had spent the entire two months just on a few lines. That was the last time I opened a Bible until I met my husband, Glen, twenty years later.

Fortunately, Glen gifted me the *Life Application Study Bible*, written in modern-day English. I was able to easily understand it and I enjoyed the thorough explanations at the bottom of each page. Sometimes I got so excited that I would spend an hour copying down verses that inspired me. One day I decided to open my Bible to whatever page it fell to and read from James 1:12, "God blesses the people who patiently endure testing." It was the exact message I needed at the time. Receiving this message led me on a journey to the understanding and experience of faith. Eventually, I became part of a prayer chain and later decided to write this book. I believe that God directed me to write this book in order to help me understand the true meaning of wisdom and faith and to help others to do the same. Even if I had never completed or published this book, I have gained more insight and experience about living my life on faith than I would ever have imagined possible.

The Stories, Lessons and Purpose of this Book

I have always learned well from stories that clearly taught me a lesson and were easy to remember. They were like paintings that stayed in my mind. Remembering them seemed to help me in my life, especially in crisis situations. Each story in this book is followed by a lesson, as well as thought-provoking questions to answer. These personal questions support you in applying the lesson to your life.

It is best to read the stories in the order they are presented. However, each chapter is in itself complete, making it possible for you to read a story anywhere in the book and have it make sense. In addition, you might want to experiment with family and friends by getting together and reading a chapter aloud. Afterwards, you could ask everyone to write answers to the questions at the end of the story and have them discuss their answers in small groups.

The purpose of this book is to give you a new perspective about the freedom of choice you can have in your life. Through numerous stories and lessons learned, this book can help you understand how to both develop and deepen your faith so that you can truly "look to this day," rather than live in the past or the future. May these stories inspire you and assist you on your path from fear to freedom and from doubt and worry to faith, love, and joy.

What is faith?

It is the confident assurance that what we hope for is going to happen.

It is the evidence of things we cannot yet see.

—Hebrews 11:1

Trust

Many of us have had some type of trauma or bad experience in our lives that led to our not trusting ourselves or not trusting others. The first strong memory I have relating to trust dates back to when I was five years old. My parents told me they were taking me to see a cartoon show. I felt quite excited about it. They parked near a very large building and took me inside. The next thing I remember I was lying face up on a large bed with a very bright light shining overhead. Suddenly, my face was covered with something that smelled horrible. I didn't learn until much later that I had been put to sleep with ether. Instead of seeing cartoons that day as I had expected, my tonsils had been taken out. What a terrible shock!

Back then, many parents, including mine, thought it was best not to be honest with their children about going to the hospital. They thought they were saving their children from experiencing fear. I had believed what my parents told me, only to find out later that they had lied to me. This event greatly affected my ability to trust others. Unfortunately my mistrust of others lasted for many years. This mistrust seemed to lead to a pattern of having other people repeatedly deceive me and to having an experience of shock by their deception.

The Lesson

Do you believe that what you don't know won't hurt you? Think about how this belief could cause you to avoid seeing or acknowledging the truth about people and/or situations. Some of us even deny what is really going on so we can avoid pain and pretend that others, as well as ourselves, are trustworthy. We don't want to believe that anyone, especially those we love, would knowingly distort the truth and manipulate us into believing something that is untrue. We want to trust others so much that we often stay in denial, going against our immediate instincts. This can cause us to be hurt and betrayed because we don't have our eyes open from the beginning. The reality is that some people are honest and can be trusted while other people are not trustworthy. Recognizing this truth is essential.

Applying the Lesson

1a. Do you currently assume people are trustworthy or untrustworthy?

Trustworthy _____ Untrustworthy _____

b. What do you base this assumption on? _____

_____

_____

_____

_____

_____

c. Have peoples' actions proven to you that your assumption is accurate?

Yes _____ No _____

d. Give a brief example _____

_____

_____

_____

2. Think about your life. What major events or memories stand out in your mind that may have led to your not trusting others? Write them here:

_____

_____

_____

_____

3. At the present time, how does your mistrust of others affect your personal and business relationships? _____

_____

_____

_____

_____

_____

_____

4a. Has your trust been restored in some way over the years?

Yes _____ No _____

b. If so, what happened to restore it? _____

_____

_____

_____

c. Establishing trust in your relationships leads to deeper connections with people. If your trust has been restored, have you experienced a deeper intimacy in your relationships?

Yes _____ No _____

d. Briefly explain your answer _____

_____

_____

_____

_____

_____

Changes in attitude never come easily.

The development of love and compassion is a wide
round curve
that can be negotiated only slowly,
not a sharp corner that can be turned all at once.

It comes with daily practice.

—Dalai Lama

About Attitude

Most of us have seen or heard Chuck Swindoll's saying, "The longer I live, the more I realize the impact of attitude on life. The remarkable thing is we have a choice every day regarding the attitude we will embrace for that day. We cannot change our past. We cannot change the fact that people will act in a certain way. We cannot change the inevitable. The only thing we can do is play on the one thing we have and that is our attitude. I'm convinced that life is 10 percent what happens to me and 90 percent how I react to it. And so it is with you. We are in charge of our attitudes." Research has shown that our minds have a strong influence on our health. The following is a summary of a true story exemplifying the impact attitude can have on our well-being.

Several years ago a man named George fell deeply in love with a woman. They seemed to be compatible in every phase of their lives, both business and personal. At a certain point in their relationship, when they were discussing marriage, George started to wonder why this woman was always busy on Monday nights. Finally, his curiosity got the better of him and he decided to investigate. He noticed the same car was parked in his girlfriend's driveway almost every Monday evening. Upon extensive investigation, he discovered she had been having an affair with a married man for fourteen years. He confronted her with this extremely upsetting information and asked her to make a choice. He was willing to give her thirty days to decide between himself and the other man. She begged George to at least be friends with her, but he rejected this idea because he loved her too much. At the end of the thirty days, she admitted she was unwilling to give up her relationship with the other man. From that time on, he built up a hatred towards her and towards the other man, due to the deception. George became ill and his illness worsened. As the weeks went on, he considered entering a hospital. At that very moment, it suddenly occurred to him why he had become so sick. He realized it was due to the woman's deception and his disgust about it. He immediately made the decision that the relationship was over and he wasn't going to let it hurt him anymore. To his surprise, the illness disappeared within two days and he became strong again. George's attitude had a profound effect on him. Changing his attitude may have actually saved his life.

The following is a true story about a young woman in her mid-twenties from South America, and the impact her attitude may have had on her mother's health. Upon meeting Maria, I was enchanted with her beautiful laugh and smiling eyes. Many people who knew her might have thought, "If only I could have been that lucky and had such a happy life." Hanging around a person like Maria, who had such an uplifting attitude, would make anyone feel good. No matter how terrible a day you might have had, just being around her automatically cheered you up.

It was a surprise for me to discover that life wasn't always a bowl full of cherries for her. Maria shared with me the following experience: "Five years ago my mom went to the hospital with a very serious illness. Nobody knew what was going to happen, even the doctor. When my mom left our house, she was so pessimistic about her recovery that she prepared everything for us, fearful she would be unable to come back home. But I knew that couldn't happen to her or to our family. I knew we were strong enough to change the situation. I decided to think positive things and I really trusted in those things. Then I prayed to God. So it happened just how I wanted it to happen. She came home. That was five years ago. I am so happy she is okay now."

The Lesson

George's attitude had a profound effect on him. He realized that he was only hurting himself by holding onto resentment and anger. Maria made a choice to think positively about her mother's recovery. Her attitude apparently contributed to her mother's healing.

Our attitude not only influences our mental and physical health, but also has a strong impact on our personal and business relationships. Although life offers no guarantees, keep in mind the following anonymous quotation "The remarkable thing is we have a choice every day regarding the attitude we will embrace for that day."

Applying the Lesson

1. On a scale of one to ten, what impact do you think attitude can have on a person's life?

    1   2   3   4   5   6   7   8   9   10

2a. Would you say you have a positive attitude about life the majority of the time?

    Yes _____ No _____

b. If not, what thoughts cause you to feel negative and/or pessimistic? (For example, I'll never be able to make enough money to live the lifestyle I desire. Who could love me? It's impossible to have a friend you can really trust. Maybe I'm just not capable of having a healthy, loving relationship. I'll never be understood.)

_____

_____

_____

_____

3. Complete these sentences using the words "optimistic" or "pessimistic" to describe the attitudes of the following people.

   a. My mom was more _____ than

      _____ about life.

   b. My dad was more _____

      than _____ about life.

   c. My best friend is a/an _____

      person most of the time.

   d. My spouse (or significant other) is _____

      most of the time.

4. In what ways do you believe your parents influenced your attitude?

   _____

_____

_____

_____

5a. Describe one incident when your attitude was positive and a good result happened.

_____

_____

_____

_____

b. Describe one incident when you had a negative attitude and a negative result then followed.

_____

_____

_____

6a. What types of activities influence your attitude in a positive way? (For example, watching a comedy, exercising, playing tennis, playing a musical instrument, going to a concert, talking with a close friend, taking a vacation, buying a new outfit, listening to uplifting tapes, doing a small art project, reading an inspiring biography, going to church or temple, etc.)

_____

_____

_____

_____

b. What enjoyable, fun activities are you willing to participate in or do more often?

_____

_____

_____

_____

c. Can you see how doing these activities could influence your attitude as well as your energy and motivation?

Yes _____ No _____

Suggestion: Schedule some of these activities in your calendar this month.

7. Keep a journal by your bed or put a bookmark in this page with a reminder to answer the following questions at the end of this week:

a. Describe the experience you had while engaging in some of the activities you listed in 6b.

_____

_____

_____

_____

b. How did these activities affect your attitude? _____

_____

_____

c. Now that you know what can influence your attitude in a positive way, how can you integrate this information into your life now?

_____

_____

_____

8. List a few other ideas you may have for living a more joyful life.

_____

_____

_____

_____

If instead of a gem, or even a flower, we should cast the gift of a loving thought into the heart of a friend, that would be giving as the angels give.

—George MacDonald
19th Century Novelist, Poet, Minister

The Peach Tree

As far back as I can remember, I have always loved flowers. My mom told me that when I was a little girl, I would often come home with a bouquet for her, picked from the neighbor's yard. Flowers, I believed, belonged to everyone. Ever since then, they have remained important to me. My home reflects this, with flower paintings hanging on the walls, and fresh flowers on my dining room table. This love for flowers led to a very meaningful experience for me several years ago.

It was a beautiful, sunny, spring day in San Diego, California. As I walked down the street, noticing the landscaping of each home, a gorgeous peach tree caught my eye. Each blossom was so bright, alive, and colorful. A smile came immediately to my face. As I was admiring the tree a young girl drove up and stepped out of her car. I told her how beautiful the tree was. She enthusiastically told me that five years earlier her mom had planted a peach pit in a small cup and after it had grown a while she planted it outside expecting it to bear fruit. Her husband, however, told her that it would never bear fruit. She didn't listen and told him it would bear more fruit than he could imagine. With a big grin, the young girl confided to me, "That's exactly what happened!"

Hearing this was so inspiring to me that I started crying. Too often in my life I had listened to people with negative outlooks and let it effect me. At that moment something powerful happened. I made a decision to go for what I most cared about in my life, rather than listen to other people's opinions. Little by little I started to surround myself with supportive people. Since making that choice, I have been able to see that beautiful peach tree and taste its abundant sweet fruit over and over again.

The Lesson

Our thoughts are very important. We need to be constantly aware of what we tell ourselves as well as what others tell us. A strong connection exists between our thoughts and the results in our lives. In addition, surrounding ourselves with as many supportive people as possible definitely makes a difference. Being a supportive person ourselves is just as important.

Think about all those times you get impatient with yourself, let others discourage you, stop taking action toward your vision and settle for what you think you can have. When that happens we are just like the husband saying, "There will never be any fruit on the tree."

Look deeply within yourself at what you truly want and know that you can have it no matter what others say.

Applying the Lesson

1. When other people discourage you, do you have a greater tendency to give up on your dreams or do you continue to pursue them?

    Tendency to give up _____ Continue to pursue _____

2. What are a few factors that assist you to pursue your dreams rather than give them up?

_____

_____

_____

3a. Describe an incident when your ideas were criticized.

_____

_____

_____

_____

b. What was your reaction?

_____

_____

_____

c. If you had it to do over again would you have responded differently?

Yes _____ No _____

d. Describe your new response.

_____

_____

_____

4a. Do you have people in your life who support you and your dreams?

Yes _____ No _____

b. If not, find a person who can support you. After you tell them your needs, ask them if they would make a commitment to assist you. For example, they could:

    1. Get together with you and help you with your action plan.

    2. Have them call you once a week at a specific time to ask what actions you have taken and to give you any further suggestions you may need.

    3. Encourage you to avoid negative, discouraging people—even if they are family or friends—helping you to see the benefit of having positive-minded people around you.

    4. Give you constructive criticism and feedback as needed.

Great works are performed not by strength,
but by perseverance.

—Samuel Johnson
18th Century English Critic,
Essayist, Biographer, Poet

Do Dead Ends Stop You?

One day I decided to take some time off with a friend of mine, Camille. It was a gorgeous, sunny, warm Sunday afternoon typical of San Diego's spring weather. After driving to La Jolla Cove, we found a parking spot overlooking the ocean. Camille was so inspired by the beauty of the coast that she began skipping along the sidewalk as if she were three years old. Her playfulness was so contagious that I felt like her three year old playmate, having as much fun as the seals swimming nearby.

After a forty-five minute walk along the ocean, we descended some stairs leading to the beach. We started walking over some large rocks and then Camille tried jumping over a two foot crevice. Unfortunately, her foot slipped on a wet rock and she fell. I wish I'd had a camera at that moment. I knew she hadn't hurt herself, but she looked so funny with her hands on one side of the crevice and her feet on the other, like a bridge. The workmen in a house nearby started laughing, but this didn't phase Camille in the least. Instead, she looked up at them and asked, "Why don't you help me?" I ran over to her and in seconds she stood up, laughing about the whole experience.

Slowly but surely, the surf started rolling in closer and closer to our feet. I suggested we either turn back or see if we could climb up the rocks and go through one of the apartment buildings that faced the street. Camille advised going through one of the apartment buildings.

First we followed a zig-zag walkway towards the back of the building and found a locked door. We looked around further and found a door that was ajar. It opened onto a construction site. We walked through the door and up a flight of stairs only to find another locked door. At this point most people would have turned around and returned to the beach. I was definitely ready to do that. The surf was starting to rush in fast and furious and I was afraid we would be stuck in the building. Camille had a different idea, however.

"Come on," she encouraged. "Let's go through this other door." I nervously told her that I was game. I didn't trust myself to find my way alone, but I trusted Camille because she was so confident. In we went, walking down a number of corridors, only to find a restroom, but no exit. There wasn't another soul in sight. By then my heart was pounding. In the past I would have given up. Instead, I walked around the hallway and luckily found someone to answer our most important question: "WHERE IS THE EXIT?" Following his directions, we found an elevator and took it to the correct floor. We were ecstatic to see the EXIT sign! Whew! What a relief! Out we bounced, safely on our way.

The Lesson

No matter how many obstacles or "dead ends" get in your way, if something really matters to you, continue to take action. Sometimes it takes longer than you think it should. That is when it's easy to lose patience and give up.

Most of us are constantly distracted by problems and short-term demands such as the telephone, eating, errands, kids, etc. We can either allow these things to get in our way and then rationalize why we can't do something, or we can take actions that support our choices best. Some of us get very impatient and quit before we give something a real chance. Many of us want a guarantee that things will turn out well. When we realize there are no guarantees, we often stop taking actions.

In order to invent our future, we must be willing not to know how it will all turn out. When it looks like there are dead ends and nowhere to go, we can either get scared and quit, or we can notice how we feel, remember what it is we want, and keep going. That is how architects build buildings, musicians compose songs, and artists paint paintings.

Applying the Lesson

1a. If you put yourself into this story would your tendency have been to turn around and quit?

Yes _____ No _____

b. When have you stopped yourself from going after something you really wanted because of fear of the unknown, fear of failure or fear someone wouldn't like you?

_____

_____

_____

2a. Think of a time when there was no stopping you. Briefly describe that situation.

_____

_____

_____

b. What allowed you to keep going, in spite of any fear you may have had?

_____

_____

_____

_____

3. Who can you ask to support you in making sure you continue to take effective actions towards your aspirations?

_____

_____

_____

_____

_____

4. Try the following experiment. You will need another person, about your height, and a sign (at least 8"x 10") set on an easel, a chair or a table so that it's high enough for you to see. Write on the sign: $1 million. The object of this experiment is for you to reach the sign. There are two parts to the experiment:

a. Ask the person you selected to stand halfway between you and the sign (about four feet). Then ask her to stand facing you as if to stop you. Ask her to bring her arm out to her side, shoulder-height, and have her get ready to try to stop you from reaching the sign.

b. Now you are going to try to walk to the sign while focusing on your friend's outstretched arm which is trying to stop you.

c. After doing this, answer this question: Did you reach the sign or did your friend stop you?

_____

_____

d. Now you are going to try to walk to the sign, but this time you are going to focus on the $1 million sign and on getting to the sign, rather than on your friend stopping you.

e. After doing this answer this question: Did you reach the sign?

Yes _____ No _____

If you reached the sign this time, but not the first time, write your opinion about what you think made the difference.

_____

_____

_____

_____

_____

_____

Black to White

Black to white
    Going through a maze
        Not knowing

Thinking there's no exit
    Getting scared and frightened
        Wanting to turn back

Doubting, doubting, doubting
    Praying for an answer
        Impatiently waiting
            Wanting to give up

Learning
    Finally seeing new colors
        New ways of thinking

Hands stretched out to you
    God's hands
        God's presence
            Learning FAITH

Dare you believe?
    Is it worth the risk?

Remembering the joy,
    the child in you

 the playfulness.
  the love.

"Yes!"
 It's worth the risk
  of not knowing how it will all turn out.

Being free
 Being able to see
  Beyond the illusions

A path lit just for you
 It's the right path
  Not the one you were told you had to walk on
   The one you choose to walk on.

What a blessing! Thank you, God!

Carol and grandmother

Joyful at Ninety-Eight

Most people never imagine living to be eighty years old, much less ninety-eight. On my grandmother's ninety-eighth birthday (11/11/97), I asked her what helped her to live to such a ripe old age. She began giggling like a little girl and told me that she just decided to quit worrying. She was able to do this because one day she suddenly forgot what she was worried about. I was completely taken by surprise at this simple, yet wise, answer.

One month after her birthday, my Grandma Betty died, but her joyful spirit continues to live with me. I am so grateful that a few years earlier my brother videotaped an interview with her. This video captured her sense of humor, her happy memories of the past, and her passion and zest for life.

My grandmother was a pioneer. At age four, she moved with her family from London, England, to New York City. A short time later she was kidnapped. Fortunately, she was found within a week, but her parents decided that America was not the place for them, so they moved back to England. A few years later my grandmother's uncle convinced them to return to the United States.

At eighteen years of age my grandmother met and married my grandfather. In the late 1930s, when my grandmother was forty, she headed for Southern California, leaving my grandfather behind to tend to their five dress shops. After she opened a new dress shop, she sent for my grandfather. All her life she designed and made her own clothes, and even at eighty-five, she was still proudly modeling them in fashion shows.

Her very favorite memory was the day she celebrated her nineteenth birthday. She used to joyfully tell me, "The church bells were ringing, the factory whistles were blowing, and people were actually dancing in the streets at four o'clock in the morning. I couldn't believe it!" Then she found out the celebration was because World War I had ended. "Can you imagine?" she excitedly shared. "Right on my birthday, November 11, 1918. I will never forget it!"

The Lesson

Joyful memories and having an active, healthy life mean a lot in your later years. Decide to quit worrying! Look back at all the things you've spent hours, and even days, worrying about. How many of these "worries" ever actually happened? Why not make the best of every day and every year of your life so that you, too, will have many beautiful memories.

Applying the Lesson

The following questions are lots of fun to discuss with others, especially family and friends:

1a. Did you ever personally speak to someone who was healthy and in their eighties or nineties?

Yes _____ No _____

b. Was it a positive experience? Yes _____ No _____

c. If it was positive, in what ways did it change your idea about living a long, healthy life?

_____

_____

_____

_____

_____

2a. How many of your grandparents are alive? _____

b. How old are they?

_____

c. How many of your grandparents did you get a chance to know? _____

_____

d. Describe a positive experience that you had with one or more of your grandparents.

_____

_____

_____

_____

_____

3a. Do you have any special memories of some positive advice your grandparents gave you?

Yes _____ No _____

b. Describe what type of advice they gave you and how it may have been helpful to you.

_____

_____

_____

_____

_____

4a. Set aside about fifteen to thirty minutes. Turn on some relaxing music and find a quiet place to write (indoors or outdoors). At the top of a blank sheet of paper, write the title "Joyful at Ninety." Then close your eyes and begin to imagine yourself healthy, active, balanced, doing what you enjoy, looking and feeling ageless.

b. Next, write down your description of the "ideal life" you imagined leading at ninety years old (as if it were already happening). After you finish, have fun reading it to someone. You might want to type it up and update it as new ideas come to you.

5. *Further Suggestions*

a. Borrow or buy a book on centenarians and read some of the biographies.

b. Find a role model who represents a person who is successfully aging. If you cannot find one, visit an active Senior Program at a community college or elsewhere. Interview them and find out what makes them joyful. If you would like to, ask them for lunch, a movie, a concert, or whatever would be fun for both of you.

Why Worry About Tomorrow?

—Clay Harrison

Why worry about tomorrow
And the rising of the sun,
Or anguish over past mistakes
That cannot be undone?

Why waste life's precious moments
On things that bruise the heart,
When today is ours to fashion
Into a work of art?

Today comes but once, my friend,
It never can return–
So use it wisely while you can,
There's a lesson you may learn.

Let history record the past
And tomorrow come what may,
Be content to do your best
With what you have today!

Appearance Counts,

Doesn't It?

Appearance was once of major importance in my life. Among my earliest memories is when my first girlfriend suddenly messed up my hair and angrily yelled, "I can't stand your hair because it always looks so perfect!" I was shocked, hurt, and very confused by her reaction. At nine years old I thought that if I looked good, then people wouldn't criticize me (especially my mother).

From childhood through adolescence my mother neatly laid my clothes out on my chair each morning. For some reason, I never questioned why she did this for me. Although I don't remember being asked what I wanted to wear, it may have happened occasionally. Appearance was of utmost importance to my mom. She always made sure she looked good, and she was adamant that I looked good, too.

When I was sixteen, our family moved into a new house. Soon after, one of my mother's friends dropped by unannounced. I had my hair up in rollers, and I recall hearing the doorbell ring and my mom calling out that it was her friend, Sylvia, coming to take a tour. I didn't have enough time to get to my bedroom without Sylvia seeing me in my rollers. My heart started beating rapidly.

I was really scared that I would be seen looking terrible. Realizing how embarrassed I would feel if Sylvia saw me in my rollers, I decided to hide in the broom closet, praying that Sylvia would soon leave. I could hear my mom and her friend chatting just on the other side of the closet door. All of a sudden, Sylvia asked to see the inside of the broom closet. I was terrified and my thoughts began to race. "Oh no! What should I do?" When I heard the handle turn, my heart jumped. The door opened and I dashed out and ran to my bedroom hoping Sylvia hadn't seen me in my rollers. What a nightmare! To this day, I can hardly believe that I would do such a crazy thing, but that really proves how important my appearance was to me at the time.

I was almost twenty-one when I got married. I recall feeling extremely insecure and nervous about shopping for clothes by myself. Having to make a final decision was very uncomfortable and difficult for me. However, if I took a friend along, I felt more secure deciding what clothing to buy. Appearance continued to be a major concern. I needed feedback to help me make the "right" choice. Only after receiving this advice from others did I feel assured that I wouldn't be judged or criticized.

The Lesson

To avoid the pain and discomfort of others criticizing us, we try to look good. We are actually attempting to manipulate others to approve of us by making ourselves look a certain way. For example, some people will never answer the door without wearing makeup. Others wouldn't think of allowing someone to visit unless their house was immaculate. Many people get so addicted to looking perfect that they cannot miss a day or two at the gym. They conclude that they have to look a certain way just to gain approval. This can lead to extreme disorders, such as anorexia or bulimia, which are potentially life-threatening.

When you must look good because you fear rejection, you

have no freedom to be yourself. The next time you find yourself having to impress someone, ask yourself if you really want to manipulate them into approving of you. How would you feel if someone tried to manipulate you this way? The reality is that no matter what you do, some people will like you and some won't. You won't die from rejection. In fact, the pain of not being yourself can cause you to feel much worse.

Applying the Lesson

1. In what ways was appearance important in your childhood?

_____

_____

_____

_____

_____

_____

2. What ways do you seek approval through your physical appearance?

_____

_____

_____

3a. Were you ever made to feel embarrassed by your looks?

Yes _____ No _____

b. If you answered "yes," briefly describe what happened.

_____

_____

_____

_____

_____

c. Were you ever criticized about your appearance?

Yes _____ No _____

d. If yes, briefly describe an incident when this occurred.

_____

_____

_____

_____

_____

e. Do you find yourself trying to avoid criticism?

Yes _____ No _____

_____

_____

_____

f. If yes, what is wrong with having people criticize you (other than their disapproval or rejection)? _____

_____

_____

4a. Do you think you need to look good all the time (i.e., wear makeup or nice clothes to the grocery store, have the perfect figure when you go swimming, etc.)?

Yes _____ No _____

b. Give one or more examples of the above.

_____

_____

_____

_____

5a. How often are you conscious of your weight?

_____

_____

b. Do you diet? Yes _____ No _____

c. What do you think is motivating this behavior?

_____

_____

_____

d. Could it be a need for your own approval?

Yes _____ No _____

e. Others' approval? Yes _____ No _____

f. Who specifically do you want approval from?

_____

6a. If appearance is of utmost importance to you try one of the following experiments:

1. Go without lipstick for one week.

2. Answer the doorbell without wearing make-up and/ or without brushing your hair.

3. Wear gardening clothes to the grocery store.

b. If this experiment does not suit you, think of an idea of your own that relates to your fears of not looking good. What experiment do you plan to try?

_____

_____

c. If you tried one of the above suggestions (or your own idea), write about what happened and how you felt.

_____

_____

_____

d. What reaction did you perceive from others?

_____

_____

_____

e. How did you feel at the end of the experiment?

_____

_____

_____

A smile
happens in a flash,
but the memory of it
can last a lifetime.

—Anonymous

Life is Beautiful

Have you ever heard someone expressing so much love, gratitude and appreciation that you just burst out crying because you were so touched? This happened to me as I watched Roberto Benigni exuberantly jump on top of chairs and leap to the stage to receive the Academy Award for Best Actor and Best Director of the movie *Life is Beautiful* on March 21, 1999.

I was quite surprised by my reaction. As I listened to him speak, what really got to me was seeing the deepest of love this man had for everyone, his childlike joy, how he knew he had not done it alone, how he believed that the support of everyone was what made the world work, and how he expressed that if you have faith, dreams come true. My heart was so touched. Just listening to him speak so genuinely and passionately from his heart caused me to instantaneously connect with him, even though I had never met this man before, nor seen him act in a movie.

Roberto Benigni played the part of Guido in *Life is Beautiful*. Guido was a charming but bumbling waiter, gifted with a very colorful imagination and an irresistible sense of humor. This extraordinary tale exemplifies how he had created a beautiful life with the wife and young son he so adored, and how he had this life threatened by World War II and the Nazi concentration camps. Rather than surrendering to hopelessness and despair, he continued to use his strengths, his imagination and his sense of humor in the face of an unthinkable and devastating fate. He did this so that his son, his wife and he could live the precious moments they had left as fully as possible.

Passion! Passion for life! Passion for people! Living that passion! That was the essence and spirit of the character Roberto Benigni played. I believe that the message he wanted people to get was that no matter what the circumstances or the calamity, our precious life can be beautiful. We are the ones who have the power to make it that way.

The Lesson

When we feel, we connect to people. We love and are loved. We are excited and passionate about people and about life itself. Yes, life has its pain. But by trying to protect ourselves from pain, we disconnect ourselves from others. We are unable to give and receive love at the deepest of levels. Our natural joy cannot be felt or expressed. When we open ourselves to Roberto's joyful attitude that "Life is Beautiful," our world becomes a better place.

Applying the Lesson

1a. Name something you are passionate about.

_____

b. How often do you spend time involved in this activity?

_____

c. Rather than putting it on the back burner, are you willing to make it one of your priorities?

Yes _____ No _____

d. If not, why not?

_____

_____

_____

_____

_____

2. Find some joyful people to be around. Being around joyful, alive, fun-loving people like Roberto Benigni, is infectious. Their joy and sense of being alive will begin to spill over into your own life.

3. Watch the video *Life is Beautiful* starring Roberto Benigni. Discuss your reaction to it with a friend or family member. Then make some notes.

   Note: This movie can be seen in Italian with English subtitles. Since Roberto's native language is Italian, this version may exemplify even more the true essence of Guido, which is the part Roberto played.

   My reaction to the movie: _____

   _____

   _____

   _____

   _____

_____

_____

4a. Are you numbing yourself with too much work, food, alcohol, TV, etc.?

Yes _____ No _____

b. If yes, what do you think you may be trying to avoid?

Sadness_____?

Anger_____?

Feelings of powerlessness_____?

Grief_____?

Frustration_____?

c. Take a pen and paper. Find a quiet place and turn on some calming music. Close your eyes and take a few slow deep breaths and relax.

Write for ten minutes or more about the feeling(s) you may be trying to avoid that you described in your answer above.

_____

_____

_____

_____

d. If there is someone you can talk to who could calmly listen, ask them to help you plan some next steps (actions) that can bring you closer to feeling a sense of peace regarding your situation. An example of a next step could be for you to write the following:

I choose to have a sense of peace regarding: _____

_____

(Be specific about the situation). Read this choice every day.

Note: At first you may not believe you can achieve this, but as you read this choice daily, surprising things can happen.

On the darkest night
the stars shine
most brightly.

—Anonymous

A "Souper" Experience

All of us have formed expectations of how little, everyday, simple things are supposed to happen, like going to the post office to mail a letter, brushing your teeth, filling your tank with gas, buying flowers or having a nice dinner at a restaurant. When they continue to turn out the usual way, we never even give them a second thought. Sometimes we receive a surprise acknowledgment, a thank you card, or a few extra smiles, but those are things that happen from time to time in the course of life. At other times, our minds become open to a refreshing, new and unexpected reality.

In the midst of a somewhat stressful financial situation, an "out of the ordinary" event happened to me. One evening my husband and I had just finished having a haircut. Since it was already nine o'clock and we hadn't taken time to eat dinner as yet, I asked my husband if he would like to stop at a nearby restaurant. He wasn't very hungry, but he agreed. (As usual, he was a good sport!) The restaurant was new and very popular, but there was a one hour wait. We both decided to go across the street to another restaurant instead, where we happily waited only ten minutes.

The first table available was outside, and although it was chilly, the hostess guaranteed us that the outdoor heaters would keep us warm. Though many of the tables were filled, it felt as if we were completely alone. I looked forward to relaxing and having some quality time with my sweetheart. We ordered a yummy sun-dried tomato pizza to split, and then my husband told me he was in the mood for a big bowl of homemade soup. He decided against it, however, because it cost five dollars and we were watching our pennies very carefully at the time. I encouraged him to order it and enjoy it, and not worry about the price. "Aren't we always provided for?" I reminded him. He grinned, nodded in agreement, and went ahead and ordered the soup. We both ended up enjoying one of the best soups we had ever eaten. During our dinner we kissed and felt like we were on a romantic date.

After finishing our meal we waited patiently for our bill. To our complete surprise the waitress came over and told us that our dinner had already been paid for. We were amazed! She then informed us that a couple at a nearby table had admired the love we had for one another and decided to pay for our entire dinner. The couple also told her to wish us a life of prosperity, long life and continued joy. We asked the waitress where they were sitting and she pointed to an empty table. They had quietly vanished.

We will always wonder who this thoughtful, generous couple was and we wish we could have thanked them. This definitely exemplified what is known as "a random act of kindness." We were both so touched that tears came to our eyes. This had never happened to either of us before. I looked at my husband and told him I was so happy he had ordered the soup he wanted. God is good. He does take care of us.

The Lesson

Enjoying each moment is difficult to do if you are constantly worrying about the future. It's not very easy to have faith when there are no guarantees given that things will work out the way you would like. You can, however, practice having faith by taking baby steps. Had my husband not ordered the soup (baby step), he probably would not have been able to appreciate the fact that God does provide.

Applying the Lesson

1. Think of a time in your life when you were under pressure and you let it affect you.

   How did you react? _____

   _____

   _____

   _____

   _____

   _____

2a. *Suggestion:* If you are under emotional or financial stress, you may think you must deprive yourself 100 percent of doing anything fun until things straighten out for you. (This may end up taking longer than you expect.) Instead, choose to do something joyful at least a few times a week. This could be just taking time to pick up seashells at the beach, buying yourself your favorite ice cream, going dancing, or calling a special out-of-town friend or relative. Let go of the timetable in which you think things should happen. Remind yourself at these times that you are practicing faith. Who knows, you may end up having someone surprise you with "a random act of kindness!"

b. What situation(s) are you willing to let go of and let God take care of?

_____

_____

_____

_____

3a. On a scale of one to ten, how much faith do you think you have? (i.e. in spite of difficulties and challenges, do you really believe you will be provided for?) Circle the number:

Little faith 1 2 3 4 5 6 7 8 9 10 A great deal of faith

b. Are you surprised by your answer? Yes _____ No _____

c. If you would like to increase the above number, write down one action you could take to deepen your faith.

_____

_____

_____

4a. Has anyone done "a random act of kindness" for you?

Yes _____ No _____

b. If yes, describe briefly what happened.

_____

_____

_____

_____

_____

_____

c. Did you believe at the time that this was an answer to a prayer?

Yes _____ No _____

d. *Suggestion*: It's helpful to keep in mind those random acts of kindness that others have done for you.

5a. Have you ever done "a random act of kindness" for a stranger?

Yes _____ No _____

b. If so, describe briefly what you did. (If you did it for someone you knew, describe that instead.)

_____

_____

_____

_____

_____

c. How did you feel about doing it?

_____

_____

_____

_____

d. If you haven't ever done a random act of kindness, would you be willing to do one now?

Yes _____ No _____

But if any of you lacks wisdom,
let him ask of God,
who gives to all men generously and without reproach,
and it will be given to him.
But let him ask in faith without any doubting,
for the one who doubts is like the surf of the sea,
driven and tossed by the wind.

—James 1: 5-8

At Rest

Have you ever felt scattered, not knowing which end is up? Did you ever stop trusting yourself to make the right choices, thinking you had to turn to others for answers? That was my state of mind two years after my marital separation. At the time I was the stressed mother of two teenagers.

During this period of time, I was invited to attend an art exhibit. I was attracted to a large, beautifully framed sketch of a young woman, deep in thought. Her head was resting on her folded arms and she looked relaxed and at peace. The name of the sketch was *At Rest* by Gerrit Grève. For many years I longed to feel like the green-eyed woman in the picture, so I knew I had to buy it. I had the strange idea that if I stared at the woman in the picture often enough, I might feel like her.

Within a month of buying the sketch, I enrolled in a course that taught people how to create what they wanted in their lives. By the end of the course, six weeks later, I had created some wonderful results. At the same time, my final divorce papers arrived. To my pleasant surprise, I actually began to feel like the woman in the drawing—relaxed and at peace.

Since that time, prayer has helped me feel at peace, especially when my husband or a dear friend, prays with me. It allows me to let go of upsetting situations and gives me the confidence that everything will be taken care of in God's timing and in His way.

Other things that have helped me feel peaceful are:

> Writing a list of things I am grateful for (however small they may be).
>
> Playing the piano.
>
> Walking at the ocean.
>
> Listening to inspiring speakers, whether live or on audio tape.
>
> Listening to Mozart's music.
>
> Listening to relaxing, beautiful songs, including classical guitar.
>
> Cooking or baking with my children.
>
> Calling a special friend.
>
> Watching young children play or having them sing to me.
>
> Having a massage, especially a Thai massage.
>
> Watching a sunset.
>
> Playing and listening to a zither (lap harp).

Several years ago I had the opportunity of spending twenty-four hours in silence with a group of twelve people. Never having attempted such a feat before, it was amazing to find how thoroughly enjoyable it was to sit, walk, and even eat while in complete silence. Driving home at the end of this retreat, I recall being stunned by how much brighter and more colorful the flowers and trees appeared. This felt very peaceful. For the very first time it was easy to understand the meaning of the phrase, "Silence is golden."

The Lesson

It's very important to take nurturing time for ourselves on a daily basis. By creating rest, quiet, and joy for yourself, your relationships will improve. You will have more energy, improved health, and an inner calmness. In the long run, your creative juices will flow into many areas of your life.

Applying the Lesson

1. On the average, how many hours per week do you nurture yourself (i.e. take time to do things for yourself that you enjoy)?

2. On a scale of one to ten, how peaceful do you feel on a daily basis? (Circle the answer)

    1   2   3   4   5   6   7   8   9   10

3a. Make a list of things that have helped you to relax:

    _____   _____

    _____   _____

    _____   _____

    _____   _____

    _____   _____

    _____   _____

b. What things on your list are you willing to take the time to do this week?

    _____   _____

    _____   _____

    _____   _____

c. What things are you willing to do next week?

_____   _____

_____   _____

_____   _____

d. Schedule the above things you wrote down into your calendar. If you need to spread some of them out over the next month, do so. Check here when you've finished adding them to your schedule. _____

4. Check out a web site on Tai Chi Chuan. This martial art is extremely good for slowing you down and improving your health. Videos are available with exercises. (For example, Tai Chi for Health by Lana Sprankeer or Tai Chi Chuan Long Form by Terri Dunn.)

5. Read the following poem as often as needed, especially when you find yourself hurrying and believing there's not enough time to rest or nurture yourself. The poet wrote it to go along with some soothing music he composed.

Slow Me Down, God

—Schawkie Roth

Ease the pounding of my heart
    by the quieting of my mind.

Steady my hurried pace with a vision
    of the eternal reach of time.

Creating Your Life as a Blessing

Give me, amid the confusion of the day,
      the calmness of the everlasting hills.

Break the tensions of my nerves and muscles
      with the soothing music of the singing streams
      that live in my memory. Help me to know
      the magical, restoring power of rest.

Teach me the art of taking minute vacations,
      of slowing down to behold a flower, to be and
      talk with a friend, to comfort an animal,
      to contemplate a few lines from a sacred book,
      and to listen to the songs of birds.

Call me to you, deep One, that I may melt evermore
      in your vast heavenly kingdom within.

Slow me down, God, and inspire me to send
      my roots deep into the soil of life's enduring
      values, that I may grow toward the stars
      and unfold my greater destiny.

—Adapted from poem by
Wilford A. Peterson

Suggestion: Put a copy of this poem on your bathroom mirror or in your office as a reminder to slow down.

I wonder why it is that we are not all kinder
to each other than we are.
How much the world needs it!
How easily it is done!

—Henry Drummond

Childhood Wounds Still Hurt

I made a business arrangement with a new client involving trading my services for hers. A few weeks later my client decided to charge me for an additional service that she had originally agreed to do for free. I felt obligated to go along with her decision, even though it made me feel very uneasy. My office manager strongly advised against it, but I assured her she had no reason to worry.

A month later, a friend of mine encouraged me to update all my financial records regarding trades and unfulfilled agreements. I decided to ask my new client to write out the balance that remained on our trade arrangement. She did this. I assumed all was well. Then, about one week later, I complained to her about some work she had done for me. I asked her if she would redo the work for free or give me credit toward future service. It slipped my mind that not long before this she had received complaints about her work from a few of her new clients. What upset her most was that her boss made her refund their money.

No sooner did I ask her to redo the work for free than she became verbally abusive. She began yelling and screaming on the telephone, accusing me of manipulation. Then she stated that she never wanted to see me or hear from me again and hung up on me. I was in absolute shock! She gave me no chance to have a normal conversation with her about what had happened.

Her reaction was so extreme that I felt like my heart had been shot with an arrow. A few weeks earlier she had lovingly given me a surprise birthday gift. What a contrast!

No amount of analysis of this situation made me feel any better about what had happened. I felt completely devastated, in pain, wounded, shocked, and depressed for a number of hours. I didn't want to be a victim, but I felt like one. I thought about my own childhood and how I had often been spanked for illogical things. One day, for example, I did not drink my pineapple juice and was spanked severely by my dad for not doing as I was told. I learned years later that my mother had been scared because my grandmother had convinced her that I would die if I did not eat enough. Somehow she got my dad to believe this too. My parents were never willing to have a logical conversation with me about it. Instead, a unilateral decision was made. They gave me no choice. I felt powerless. I felt the same way later in life whenever other people blamed me or yelled at me for things that made absolutely no sense!

Suddenly something clicked for me. The shock I felt when my client had hung up on me and wouldn't discuss the situation was actually a repeat of my above-mentioned childhood experiences. Now it seemed that a unilateral decision was made once again and I had no choice about it. As I became conscious of the role I had been playing in this type of situation, I began to take responsibility for my own behavior and to react differently. I realized that I had been afraid to tell my client that I didn't want to change our initial agreement because I feared she would get angry at me and think I wasn't being fair. No wonder I felt like a victim. This new realization opened my eyes to taking responsibility for my actions and reactions. Eventually, I no longer experienced myself as a victim in my relationships, and was able to communicate my true feelings, needs and desires.

The Lesson

When we feel like a "poor me" victim and blame other people for our misfortune or upsets, it's best for us to stop and think about what part we may have played in causing the situation. As children we are often victims of our circumstances. As adults we have a choice. If we blame others and haven't learned that we have freedom of choice, painful situations often reoccur. Recognizing we have repeating patterns is the first step in dealing with these situations.

Applying the Lesson

1a. Do you recognize any repetitive victim patterns you have?

Yes _____ No _____

b. If so, describe briefly what usually happens. _____

_____

_____

_____

_____

2a. Have you ever had a shock, as described in this story?

Yes _____ No _____

b. If so, before this shock happened, were there any red flags that you didn't see or chose not to see? Yes _____ No _____

c. If so, what were they?

_____

_____

_____

d. Why do you think you didn't notice these red flags, or chose to ignore them?

_____

_____

_____

_____

_____

e. Do you think you should have known better?

Yes_____ No_____

Forgiving yourself is important. Remind yourself that you couldn't have known before you knew.

3a. Is there anyone you are still blaming for something that is happening right now, or for something that happened in the past? Yes_____ No_____

b. If so, how does it benefit you to remain feeling like a victim (i.e. powerless)?

_____

_____

_____

_____

c. Can you see what part you played in saying "yes" to becoming a victim?

Yes _____ No _____

d. Why did you say "yes"?

_____

_____

_____

_____

_____

4. If this were your best friend, what advice would you give to assist her in powerfully creating what she wanted from this situation?

_____

_____

_____

_____

Life is like a motor car.
A motor car can be used
to travel great heights,
But most people lie in
front of it, allow it to
drive over them, then
blame it for the accident.

—Anthony de Mello
Jesuit, Spiritual Teacher, Author

Nurturing Your Mind,

Spirit and Soul

I love listening to the sound of the ocean
as the waves roll in,
Disappearing into the sand.
Suddenly new waves appear out of nowhere
Repeating the same process,
Rolling in,
Disappearing into the sand.

Flags waving in the breeze.
The sun sparkling on the cool water.
Tiny sailboats gliding by in the distance.

Being at the ocean can nurture your mind, spirit and soul.

A child kicks a colorful beach ball
and gleefully runs after it.
Another young child smiles,
free from worry as he runs to his mommy and daddy.

How little time we take to just be,
To breathe in the fresh ocean air,
To listen to the birds,
To walk in nature,
To feel, hear, see, touch and smell its God-given beauty.

Instead we're busy having expectations of people,
Assuming they should be a certain way.
They should understand how we feel.
They should keep their appointments with us.
(After all, we were looking forward to being with them)
They should communicate what's on their mind
Instead of having someone else relay the message.

Why can't they tell the truth to us directly?
Cowards! Always an excuse!
Didn't want to hurt your feelings,
Something important just came up,
Forgot about something else I had to do,
So tired, need more sleep,
Have to get up really early,
It's just not a good time,
My car broke down,
I'm under the weather,
It's raining,
Didn't have the time,
My sister just arrived,
So sorry!
Excuses, Excuses!

If you want to live a longer and healthier life
It's just not worth getting upset over these things.
Besides, aren't others free to be the way they want,
And decide what's most important to them?
And what about your freedom to be the way you want?

Being at the ocean can nurture your mind, spirit and soul.

Perhaps we take things too personally.
We need to assassinate our egos.
Bang! Bang!
Good job! Feel better?

What's really going on here?

Many of us never had the chance to make our own decisions as
    a child.
So now, when someone makes a decision for us,
We feel powerless and think we don't really count.

Assumption!

Who said you don't count?
Isn't this a conclusion you jumped to as a child?
Well, well, well! What if you believe you don't count?
What's wrong with that?
Can't you still create what you want in your life, in spite of your
    belief?

Hmmm. Never thought of that.

I love listening to the sound of the ocean
As the waves roll in,
Disappearing into the sand.
Disappearing into the sand.

The waves never worry that they don't count.
They just keep rolling in.
Rolling in.
Rolling in.

Being at the ocean can nurture your mind, spirit and soul.

The Lesson

When your mind is distressed and you're feeling angry, hurt, upset, or burned out, spending some time in nature can be very healing. Insights are often gained and a sense of peace follows.

Applying the Lesson

1a. Make a specific date with yourself to go to a favorite place in nature (woods, ocean, lake, mountains, desert, etc.). If you enjoy camping, you may want to stay overnight.

b. Be sure to bring comfortable, warm clothing (if necessary) and a journal to write in. Remember to bring some food, snacks, and plenty of water, especially if you like hiking.

c. Get comfy and take in the scenery. Breathe deeply. When you're ready to start writing, write whatever you see, feel, think, or hear. Be spontaneous. Don't censor your feelings or thoughts. Just let them flow.

d. Reread your writing and list any insights you may have received from it. _____

_____

_____

_____

e. How can these insights help you in the coming weeks?

_____

_____

_____

_____

_____

f. How did this experience nurture you? _____

_____

_____

_____

_____

g. What actions will you take over the next week or so to support your well-being, projects, relationships, etc.?

_____

_____

_____

_____

_____

Music is a holy place, a cathedral so majestic
that we can sense the magnificence of the universe,
and also a hovel so simple and private
that none of us can plumb its deepest secrets.

—Don Campbell
Author of *The Mozart Effect*

The Joy of Music

Did you ever feel your heart completely open by just listening to a piece of music? When I went to Kauai, one of the most beautiful Hawaiian islands, I fell in love with the island and the people. Before leaving I purchased some Hawaiian music. When I returned home I began listening to the music day after day. A sense of peace and harmony entered my heart, and I just wanted to sway to the music. It felt as if a gentle breeze was carrying me up to the heavens. My connection with nature seemed to deepen and I felt very loved. All I could do was smile from ear to ear. Music can affect us that way. Research has already proven the healing power of certain types of music, even for babies still in the womb.

One of my favorite Hawaiian singers is Keali'i Reichel. I especially love listening to his CD called *Lei Hali'a*, by Puakea Nogelmeier. This music is very romantic and sweet. I listened to his first song, "Lei Hali'a," which he sings in Hawaiian (this is also the name of his CD). I played it again and again for an hour. I couldn't seem to stop. I wondered what this song was all about. Then I noticed a booklet enclosed inside the CD, in which a man named Fred Krauss described the meaning of this music:

> From seed to seedling, sprout to tree, a flower blooms forth to face the sunshine and grace the air with its fragrance. With roots firmly gripping the soil and leaves protectively encircling, the gift is plucked from the grip of the branch with care by the lei maker. Through the feelings of the heart and the experienced skill of the hands, these flowers shine even more brightly on the string of the lei. Long after the life span of the individual flower, the memory of the beauty of the lei remains intact.

How true this was! If you have ever been gifted a lei, you never forget its sweet fragrance and beauty.

When I read the purpose of this CD it seemed like a beautiful prayer: "A string of songs, each conceived as a seed and given nourishment by the land, the rain, and the sun around us, is now presented to you. In the same way that each flower makes up the whole of this lei, let each song conjure a fragrance and beauty of its own . . . ." The first line of the song, named "Lei Hali'a," is repeated over and over again. This line says, "He 'ohu i ka lei hali'a," which means, "Adorned with a lei of fond recollection."

No wonder this music touched my heart. It was filled with the precious love of those who select the beautiful flowers for the Hawaiian leis and then carefully put them together. If I close my eyes, I can still see and smell the lovely lei of yellow flowers gifted to me by a special friend of mine from Kauai.

In looking back at my life, I realize how very fortunate I was to have developed a true appreciation for music. My parents often took me to classical music concerts and gave me the opportunity to study piano. It all began when I was nine years old. My best friend, Diane, decided to teach me the well-known "Chopsticks" on her piano. From then on I became interested in taking piano lessons. Fortunately, my parents were able to obtain a beautiful French provincial baby grand piano from a theater in my hometown. From the day I began taking lessons, I used to literally run home because I couldn't wait to practice. Even though I was just playing beginning pieces, I felt like a concert artist because I was playing on a baby grand piano. After one year of lessons, I auditioned for a well-known concert pianist. It was my good fortune that she was willing to teach me during my school lunch hour. My most memorable piano recital was at the age of seventeen when I played the Grieg Concerto.

Piano was one thing that I was never criticized for. No one in my family knew how to play, and they always wanted me to play for them. Playing piano helped me to achieve a more balanced, calm state. I had been a very sensitive, emotional child, and without my realizing it, piano became a meditation for me. When I played and practiced passages over and over again, I was completely in the moment. Nothing else existed at the time.

The encouragement, support and acknowledgment I received for my piano playing over the years was a true blessing. My piano teacher had so much confidence in me that when I was only seventeen she referred me two students to teach. This started me on a very enjoyable, fulfilling twenty-one year career of private piano teaching. I was fortunately able to continue this career while I raised my two children. My love and appreciation for music stems from both my piano background, my love of singing and my attending classical music concerts as a child.

The Lesson

Whether listening to music, playing an instrument, or singing, the impact music has on us is far greater than many of us realize. Experiencing music that brings us joy can greatly increase the harmony in our lives.

Applying the Lesson

1a. Have you ever played a musical instrument?

Yes _____ No _____

b. If yes, do you still play? Yes _____ No _____

c. If not, would you want to play again if you had the time?

Yes _____ No _____

d. If yes, is there a friend who would support and encourage you to get started again?

Yes _____ No _____

e. When would you like to get started?

_____

_____

2a. If you have never played a musical instrument, what instrument would you most like to learn to play?

_____

b. What's been stopping you?

_____

_____

_____

_____

_____

c. Write down some advantages of playing a musical instrument.

_____

_____

_____

d. Plan some time to go to a music store and talk to someone about taking lessons on an instrument you might enjoy playing. (If you are unsure what instrument you would prefer, discuss this with someone there. Perhaps you can set up a free lesson and try a few different instruments.)

e. Take some time to seriously consider if music lessons or singing lessons would be a joyful hobby for you.

f. If you enjoy singing, is there a choir you might like to join or a friend you'd like to do karaoke singing with?

Yes _____ No _____

3. Find a quiet place where you have room to move around (inside or outside). Put on some of your favorite music. Begin to dance in slow motion. Gradually move your entire body to the rhythm of the music. Feel whatever feelings you feel (joy, a sense of being alive, freedom, etc.).

4. Rent the video *Duets*, an inspiring movie about the joy of music.

Do not have
your concert first and tune
your instruments afterward.

Begin the day with God.

—James Hudson Taylor
Pioneer Missionary 1832-1905

Song of Faith

Tears streamed down their faces. I wondered why. All of them were in their seventies, eighties, and nineties, and I was only twelve years old at the time. My girlfriend and I had just finished singing a passionate song of faith for a large group of residents at a Jewish old folks' home. Our voices had harmonized perfectly as we sang "Father, Father." We later found out that this song had been a prayer that these people had sung in a Nazi concentration camp many years earlier. No wonder they were crying. The song brought back intensely painful memories. But, at the same time, it reminded them of how grateful and fortunate they were for the blessing of life itself. Their faith had sustained them in spite of how black their lives had been.

Imagine myself and my friend, both twelve years old, giving a brief concert for the first time. All we had hoped for was to remember the words of the song and to harmonize correctly. We had little understanding of the depth of the words we were singing.

The Hebrew title of the song is "Eli-Eli." Although I haven't sung this song since I was twelve, I was surprisingly able to recollect all the words as well as the very beautiful melody. I think it's because I loved singing the song and felt its melody deep in my soul. I can still hear my girlfriend's gorgeous soprano voice harmonizing with mine. The other reason I remembered the words is probably because of the strong impact it had on all those people present. The following are all the words to the song my friend and I sang that memorable day.

Father, Father (Eli-Eli)

Eli, Eli
Hear our plea as we pray.
Father, Father
Help us to find our way.

In these troublesome times,
In these days of woe
We turn to you dear Lord,
For we need you so.

Please help us to find
Which way we should go.
Help us to know.

Wash away our sins
Save us from the burning fire.
Father, Father
Save us from temptation.
Father, Father
You are our salvation.

Please have mercy on your children, Holy One.
Give us guidance with your wisdom, Holy One.

Give us strength,
Help us from above.
Give us hope,
Please teach us love.

Through fire and flame
And for all time.
Praise be Thy name,
Oh Lord Divine.
Sh'ma yisroel adonoi elohanu. (Hear O Israel, The Lord
Our God)
Father, Father!

The Lesson

Through song we can more easily feel emotions and therefore open our hearts to others' pain as well as joy. As a baby most of us listened to lullabies sung by our mother or played by a music box. Later in life those types of melodies remain comforting and warming to the spirit. These can be church hymns, beautiful melodies from various cultures that are sung and played on special holy days, wedding songs, etc. They continue to touch us deeply.

At one time or another we hear a song and we are immediately carried away to that place we originally heard it. Sometimes we may think of the person who sang it or danced to it with us. These special songs often help us through trauma, tragedy and loss. They uplift us and give us hope. They can fill us with love or connect us with God and with others on a deeper level than we might otherwise experience.

Applying the Lesson

1a. Describe an occasion when a song you heard or sang stayed with you over the years.

_____

_____

_____

_____

_____

_____

_____

b. Why do you think you still feel its impact?

_____

_____

_____

_____

2a. Is there someone who sang to you as a child?

Yes _____ No _____

b. If yes, and they are still alive, ask them to sing a few of those same songs to you again (if they remember them).

3a. What hymn or song can you name that is like a prayer for you? _____

_____

b. Write out the words and explain their importance to you (if you do not remember the words, try to find out what they are).

c. Ask some special people in your life what their favorite songs are and why. Write what they tell you.

_____

_____

_____

_____

_____

_____

_____

d. When was the last time you sang something special for someone you absolutely loved?

_____

_____

_____

e. Briefly describe your experience and the reaction of the person you sang to.

_____

_____

_____

_____

_____

_____

Fear is
that little dark room
where
negatives
are developed.

—Michael Prichard

Turning Point in my Life

One of the most memorable and powerful experiences of my life was at the age of thirty-seven during my first personal growth training. Three hundred people were in the room. At one point the leader asked us to raise our hand if we had a specific fear about something. I didn't hesitate to raise my hand. He immediately called on about ten people to state their specific fear.

Fear of flying, fear of abandonment, fear of being hurt, fear of failure, fear of success, and a few other fears were announced. I was one of the last ones to stand up. "Fear of being unloved," I said somewhat shyly. Within seconds the leader pointed directly at me and asked me to come up to the front of the room. A wave of fright shook my entire body. Part of me really wanted his help and part of me was very scared of being vulnerable in front of 300 people. Reluctantly, I got up from my seat and slowly walked up to the front. Although I had no idea what would happen next, I felt confident that the leader was on my side and would make sure that no harm would come to me.

This event happened so many years ago that my memory of it is quite foggy. What I vividly remember, however, is how nervous I felt when the leader asked me to sit in his director's chair, close my eyes, take a deep breath and relax. In a very compassionate voice he asked me if I wanted to get rid of my fear. I confidently nodded my head Then he asked me to visualize my fear somewhere in my body. Once I did that, he asked me to tell him where in my body it was located. I recall having a very difficult time doing that. Suddenly he yelled and said, "You are not paying attention! You are staying vague to avoid feeling pain!" My heart felt like it was being pierced by an arrow. He immediately put his hand on my arm as if he knew how I felt. Reassuring me he said, "Carol, I am not speaking to you. You are doing just fine. I am only speaking to the participants." I immediately burst out crying and couldn't stop. It was the first time in my life I had really felt understood. (This profound experience has stayed with me all my life.)

The leader asked me to once again visualize the fear in my body. Though feeling somewhat embarrassed, I told him it was located in my behind. He asked me what color it was and I told him red. Then I started to cry again and he asked me to guess what was going on. I told him it had brought back painful memories of my childhood, when I had been spanked frequently and unjustly by my father. The leader had me continue to describe the shape and color of the fear and eventually the red shape got smaller and smaller until it completely disappeared.

This was a major turning point in my life. Soon after, I began telling the truth about how I felt and what I believed. Slowly but surely this fear of being unloved no longer affected me. Friends were able to tell me how they truly felt and I began to experience intimacy and trust in my relationships.

The Lesson

When we are ready for growth and major changes in our lives, the perfect path and/or teacher often appears. Little by little we get better and better at telling the truth to ourselves and others. Once we are no longer run by our fears, our lives improve and our relationships have the chance to blossom and develop to a deeper level than ever imagined.

Applying the Lesson

1a. Briefly describe a turning point in your life.

_____

_____

_____

_____

_____

b. What actions did you take that benefited you at that time?

_____

_____

_____

_____

2a. Is there a fear or belief you have that has been keeping you from telling the truth to yourself and/or others?

Yes _____ No _____

b. If yes, what is that fear or belief? _____

_____

_____

3a. Due to our fears or beliefs we often hang on far too long in situations that are not serving us. We rationalize that there is still hope. Are you presently hanging on in a situation that is not supportive hoping it will change? Yes _____ No _____

b. Why do you think you are staying in hope when you've had more than enough red flags? (*Hint*: fear of being alone, fear there's no one else who will love you, fear of being hurt or controlled, irrational fear you will be homeless or die.)

_____

_____

_____

_____

_____

_____

4a. Write down the name of someone supportive in your life whose advice you can seek. Decide when you will speak to them.

I choose to call _____ for positive support.

b. I choose to make an appointment with _____ (friend, counselor, attorney, etc.) by _____ (date).

We must be willing
to relinquish
the life
we've planned,
so as to have
the life
that is waiting
for us.

—Joseph Campbell
Author and Mythologist

If Only I Would Have Listened

In 1987, the first time I traveled to Sedona, Arizona, I went with a group of nineteen people who had completed a ministerial training. All of us decided to go on a spiritual retreat as well as a hiking adventure. It was a wonderful trip that lasted five days. All of us bonded and became closer than we had ever been before. From that day on I knew I would revisit Sedona some day.

That day arrived in November of 1992 when I planned to spend Thanksgiving with some special friends of mine. My husband and I were invited to stay at their home in Sedona. Another friend of theirs asked to drive with us so we all made arrangements to meet. We left the day before Thanksgiving very excited about enjoying a holiday away from home.

My first day in Sedona was filled with some challenging rock-climbing and hiking with my husband, my friend, and a few other house guests. We had a fabulous Thanksgiving dinner and everything went smoothly and wonderfully until that night. When I went to bed I looked for my suitcase and couldn't find it. I asked my husband, Glen, if he had put it in the car. He soon realized he had left my suitcase in our bedroom, which was unfortunately a six-hour drive away. Intuitively, he had brought an extra jacket and an extra pair of gloves. Somehow I had a good sense of humor about it. Years ago I would have been extremely upset, but this time I just thought it was rather strange that I didn't have my suitcase. I wondered whether it had some special significance. I also remembered that before we left my mother called me and tried to talk me out of going. Her words clearly rang in my head, "Don't you need to rest? Why don't you stay home? You're always so busy!" My husband really didn't want to go either, but I was convinced that we could have a fun adventure spending our first Thanksgiving together out of town.

The day after Thanksgiving Glen and I got up extra early and went shopping for all the necessary items I had forgotten at home. Then we drove to Cathedral Rock and started to hike. It was a gorgeous, sunny day. We both were very happy to be walking in nature, breathing in the fresh air and appreciating the incredible scenery. After about a half an hour on the path, Glen decided to step down a two-foot embankment and walk over to a little brook where a young man was meditating in the bright sunlight. I told him that I would wait for him because my intuition told me that it was not safe for me to go there. All the rocks looked rather wet and I was afraid I might slip and fall. About five minutes later, my friend Barbie and about four of her house guests appeared. They asked me where Glen had gone and I told them he was exploring. All of them thought they would take a look and say hi to him. One by one, they stepped down the two-foot embankment and walked over to the brook. I could hear them all chattering and laughing, but they were out of my view. I began to feel left out because they were having such a good time. One of the women, fearful of rock climbing the day before, had surprised me by joining them. I decided that if she could go, it must be safe for me to go.

How many of us take time to tune into our intuition and listen to what it's saying? I have been teaching people for years to write down a personal question, and with pen or pencil in hand, start writing whatever words they hear in their mind. How often do I take time to do this? I do it only when I am teaching my creating classes. If I had been in the habit of listening to my intuition and following it, the following unfortunate incident would never have happened.

I took one step down, slipped on a wet rock, twisted my foot and fell. I had never felt so much pain in my life. It felt like a house had just landed on my leg. Until this time in my life I had never broken anything, but I had a strong feeling that I had just broken my leg. Someone called for the ambulance and a very sweet woman, who was also a doctor, came over and checked my leg. She confirmed that it was most likely broken.

After what seemed like centuries, the paramedics came and carried me on a stretcher to the ambulance. They tried to drive very slowly because it was an extremely bumpy road and they didn't want me to have any more pain than I already had. Everyone was really sweet and kind. It took one very long hour to get to the hospital. The doctor told me I had broken the tibia bone of my right leg. My prayers were answered, however, when they said I wouldn't need surgery. I had a circular break, which meant that I had to have a hip to foot cast for about three months. This would be followed by a knee to foot cast for another three months. The surgeon informed me that he prescribed this because he wanted to be sure my leg healed well.

I was so grateful that my sweetheart, Glen, was with me, since I had to stay in the hospital all weekend. The nurses were swamped and Glen was truly equal to at least three nurses. Finally, I was released and we drove back to San Diego.

As I lay in my bed at home, looking up at a large multi-colored watercolor painting called "Hills and Valleys," I began to feel very peaceful, even though life had dealt me a painful blow. Not only did I experience severe physical pain, but emotional pain, too. I gave up two months of teaching, a trip to San Francisco, and a first-time trip to Hawaii. My spiritual life began to deepen, however. Looking back at this experience, I realize that a lot had happened for me over those few months. Since I had to stay in bed, I listened to tapes and did nothing. Before my fall, I felt like I had to always be doing something.

My son, Drew, brought me games and we had lots of fun playing them. After I started feeling better, I invited twenty to twenty-five people to my home once a month and we had "game night." It was a lot of fun. Everyone lightened up and we all felt like kids again. Laughter is so healing!

I had never been depressed in my life before, but those first few weeks in bed gave me a thorough experience of what depression really meant. I prayed a lot with my husband and by myself. One special prayer was for a very good friend of mine to call me. He was a healer and I had lost track of him for a few years. There was a period of time when I had helped him out and he always told me that he owed me as many healings as I wanted. I thought, "Well, now's the time!"

Within a few days I received a phone call from my long-lost friend. He told me that he was moving out of town and when he tried to get rid of some phone numbers from his computer, my phone number wouldn't disappear. Since he didn't know whose it was, he decided to call before erasing the number. He was delighted to hear my message. Needless to say, he came over within a couple of days and did a fantastic healing on my leg. Then he disappeared as quickly as he had reappeared. How fortunate I felt!

After two months of using a walker, I was finally able to walk with crutches. When I began teaching English as a Second Language again, I had to wear a knee to foot cast for a few more months. Luckily, a sweet friend volunteered to drive me to school.

So much happened for me at a spiritual level during my seven month healing period. I learned to let go and let God do His work. In other words, I stopped fighting when life wasn't giving me cherries. Instead I started to carefully listen to my intuition. I will never forget this experience! It's in my cells!

Two weeks after my accident the lady who had been fearful of rock climbing came to visit me. She apologized for waiting two weeks and explained she had felt guilty. "Guilty about what?" I asked. She went on to explain that when she stepped down the two foot embankment, she realized it was dangerous and wanted to warn me not to go. For some strange reason she just kept walking and couldn't seem to turn around to tell me not to go. How uncanny it was that she also ignored listening to her intuition!

The Lesson

It's crucial to take time to listen to your heart, and to be sure to follow the messages your heart tells you. Be kind to yourself, however, when you don't listen. Blaming yourself will not serve you. Remember that you couldn't have known any better or you would have done it differently (made other choices).

I could have continued to condemn myself for not wanting to feel left out and for convincing myself it was safe to do something my intuition told me wasn't safe. However, doing so would have caused me to remain a victim. Instead, I gave myself permission to be depressed for awhile. When I was ready to heal, my son brought over some games and we had a lot of fun playing them, in spite of the pain I was in. The quality time I spent with my son was priceless. I realized I had missed a lot of precious time with him previously because I had always been too busy before my accident.

Painful, unexpected situations can be an opportunity for us to think about what is really meaningful in our lives. Then, we can make decisions that often change our lives for the better and create a whole new future.

Applying the Lesson

1. List various situations when you knew the right thing to do, but you didn't do it.

a. _____

_____

_____

b. _____

_____

_____

c. _____

_____

_____

2. What lesson did you learn from each of the above incidents?

a. _____

_____

_____

b. _____

_____

_____

_____

c. _____

_____

3. Briefly describe two situations when you followed your intuition, or prayed for an answer, and then took actions accordingly.

a. _____

   _____

   _____

b. _____

   _____

   _____

4a. What happened when you followed your intuition or prayed for an answer?

   _____

   _____

   _____

   _____

   _____

b. Were there any good surprises? Yes _____ No _____

   Comments:

_____

_____

_____

_____

_____

5. Name a decision you made that helped to create a whole new future for you (or changed the direction your life was going).

_____

_____

_____

Food for Thought: Laughter helps to heal. When you've had a reversal, rent some humorous movies, invite some friends over to visit, or have a game night. It won't take long for your spirits to be lifted.

A garden of God
is our childhood,
each day

A festival radiant with
laughter and play.

—M.J. Lebensohn

Carol at three years old.

A Child at Heart

People have often told me that I am "a child at heart." In truth, I have never felt my age (always a lot younger). A youthful appearance runs in my family. My grandmother always looked and acted at least twenty years younger than she was.

If you were to look at my refrigerator, you would see a variety of magnets holding a collage of family pictures. My favorite depicts a darling little girl, about four years old. She has curls like I used to have as a child, and a curious expression as if to say, "Oh really? Tell me more about that." Almost everyone would recognize her name, the famous and much-loved actress, Shirley Temple. What was it about her that kept me spellbound every time I watched her in a movie? It was her authenticity, her contagious laugh, her playfulness, her ability to tell the truth, and her warmth and affection. Although she was only five years old, she inspired a range of emotions in me, from deep compassion and sadness to enormous joy and happiness.

Many of us have not been able to be a child (i.e. spontaneous, joyful, silly, curious, playful, etc.). Instead, we tried to be on good behavior in order to get our parents' approval. In this way we hoped they wouldn't yell at us or spank us. Our survival seemed to be at stake. This is one of the reasons that many of us, as adults, need to feel in control. We get so scared when we think someone might leave us or stop being our friend that we manipulate ourselves into living up to their expectations. Often we end up resenting the other person.

My clients often tell me that they can't say what they think to someone because the other person will feel hurt. What is really happening is that they are the ones who are afraid of feeling hurt. Protecting ourselves from others' anger is often our major concern. How can our playful, spontaneous, free spirit burst forth if we are constantly monitoring our behavior and trying to keep the peace?

In Shakti Gawain's book, *The Path of Transformation*, she says: "It's important to get in touch with our inner child because the child is the key to our creativity. Very young children are endlessly creative because they have not yet become inhibited. They play with their imagination easily. They love to draw and paint. They sing little songs. They dance. They're magically creative beings. All of us are that way, too. We all had that magical, creative essence within us as children. As adults, we have suppressed it. As we get in touch with the child inside us, we release our creativity."

One of the most healing, nourishing, fun things one can do to experience being a child or free spirit again is to go to what's called a "play" workshop. One evening I decided to invite several of my friends and clients (aged twenty-one to seventy-seven) to attend one of these workshops with me. The facilitator of the workshop was extremely good at making everyone feel very safe and comfortable. I was absolutely amazed at the talent that my friends and clients exhibited. Everything we did was spontaneous. The little five year old inside me had the time of her life! For one of the improvisations I decided to pretend to throw a chocolate cake at someone. I squealed with delight just like Shirley Temple might have done. This play workshop was a fabulous opportunity to experience being a child again.

The Lesson

By adulthood many of us have suppressed our playfulness and spontaneity in exchange for a feeling of safety. We can become a child again by honoring the wonder of life and appreciating each new day as an adventure of discovery. As we regularly make time for ourselves to do things just for the pure joy of it, we begin to look, act and feel years younger!

Applying the Lesson

1. Here are several suggestions to help you safely get into your child role again and just have fun:

    a. Watch how children play. See their joy.

    b. Find out if there are any play workshops in your area and enroll in one. (Go with a friend or spouse, if you prefer.) Take a chance! If you don't like it you can always leave.

    c. Have a "Be a Kid" party. Dress up like a little girl or boy (wear pig-tails, etc.). Just for the fun of it, you could buy an all-day sucker. (The suckers that are so yummy and so big that they last all day.) Notice how it feels to be dressed as a child and how people react to you. Write about your experience afterwards or share about it with a supportive friend.

    d. Put up a sign in your home that says, *"Caution: Adults at play."*

    e. Buy some colored chalk (pastels) and drawing paper, turn on your favorite music, and let it inspire you to make a drawing (you don't need to show your drawings to anyone). This art experience can later be done with a group of friends.

    f. Rent a funny movie and/or rent a Shirley Temple movie.

g. Take a clown course.

h. Finger paint.

i. Play in a sandbox or make a sand castle at the beach (if there's one near you).

j. Choose your own idea.

2a. Name a few things that you loved doing as a child (riding a merry-go-round, playing with Lincoln Logs and Legos, having a lemonade stand, camping, hiking, reading, blowing bubbles, taking a bubble bath, pulling a red wagon, etc.).

_____

_____

_____

b. Would you be willing to do some of these activities again?

Yes _____ No _____

c. If so, when? _____

d. Is there someone you would like to accompany you?

Yes _____ No _____

e. If yes, who?_____

f. Which additional activities listed in the first question would you be interested in trying?

_____

3a. Have you ever gone to a play workshop? Yes _____ No _____

b. If so, did you enjoy it? Yes _____ No _____

c. What do you remember about it? _____

_____

_____

d. Would you be willing to go to one in the future?

Yes _____ No _____

4a. Were you ever taught that you had to finish your work before you could play?

Yes _____ No _____

b. Does that thought ever stop you from taking time out in your schedule to relax?

Yes _____ No _____

c. Do you think it's a waste of time to be playful?

Yes _____ No _____

d. If yes, why do you believe that being playful or taking time to relax is a waste of time?

_____

_____

5a. Were you ever made fun of or humiliated as a child?

Yes _____ No _____

b. What happened?

_____

_____

_____

c. Do you think these past experiences could be stopping you from feeling free to act silly or foolish? Yes _____ No _____

d. Are you fearful of rejection and/or the pain of looking foolish or stupid?

Yes _____ No _____

e. Recall an incident when looking foolish or silly resulted in a positive result. (For example, a new friend, a part in a play, etc.) List this positive result below.

_____

_____

_____

See With Wonder,

Be as a Child

See the sweetness children have!
    Their voices have a purity
        because they have no purpose.

They are not afraid
    that someone will think
        they are foolish.
            It doesn't matter to them.

When a child plays,
    he plays for the sake of play.
        The child is enchanted by the moment,
            the timeless time, the eternal now.

There is no purpose in the play,
    nothing to change,
        nothing to attain.

All that surrounds the child
    is a source of wonder.
        He walks and moves and looks
            with great wonder in his eyes.
A child's eyes are ever empty,

like a mirror which reflects
only what is there.
All is mysterious,
surprising, fresh, and new.

We have forgotten now,.
but one day we walked with our eyes wide
with wonder
feeling, "What's this?"
"What's that?"
"I never saw it before!"

When, like a child,
we experience life
with freshness, amazement,
and emptiness in our eyes,

then life itself
with all its mystery,
will fulfill our deepest longings.

—Amrit Desai
Author, Poet, Master Yoga Teacher

Making a Mountain

Out of a Molehill

Have you ever misplaced something, been positive you would never find it again, and then ended up finding it? Have you ever concluded there was no solution for a problem except spending a lot of money on it only to find out you were wrong? If you grew up in a home where there was at least one parent or relative who worried incessantly or got hysterical over the littlest thing, you may be suffering from a mild to severe case of "mountainitis." In other words, you blow things way out of proportion and the "molehills" of life (minor events) actually look like and feel like "mountains" (major catastrophes).

The message my mom gave me was that things would work out and not to worry. However, I often got mixed messages from her because I would hear her worry about everything, including me. Not until later in life did I realize this may have been one of the things that caused me to frequently make mountains out of molehills.

One day my husband and I were driving out of a gas station when we heard a very loud noise on the left side of our car. I opened the window, hoping the sound was coming from another car. Unfortunately the noise got louder and it sounded like something very bad had happened to one of our rear tires. We turned into the first driveway we came to so we could check it out. My husband was quite calm about it. This was his typical behavior. On the other hand, I was already somewhat hysterical. I imagined we would be unable to get home for hours, would have to call the auto club, and last but not least, would have to pay an exorbitant amount of money to fix the problem—money we definitely didn't have at the time.

To make a long story short, I had assumed the worst. Then, I discovered reality. The loud noise had been caused by a long piece of sticky packaging tape that our left rear tire had driven over. Every time the tire moved, the tape made a loud crackling sound. It took only ten seconds to unstick the tape from the tire, and the cost, of course, was free!

Another incident taught me an additional lesson about mountains and molehills. For a number of weeks my computer had been crashing and I was thinking about buying a new one. Financially, I wasn't quite ready to do that. One day I panicked because I was absolutely certain I had lost my entire database of three thousand names. I hired a computer expert to see what could be done. He was a genius. Needless to say, he was able to restore it. The day after he performed this miracle, I went to use my computer but the cursor wouldn't move. I restarted the computer only to have the cursor freeze again. After restarting it a few more times, I was 99 percent sure that my computer had moved on to computer heaven. Something major had definitely gone wrong and I would have to purchase a new computer. (Ugh!) I decided to telephone the same computer expert. He asked whether or not the mouse was plugged in. "Of course it was," I confidently replied. He then directed me to check if the connection might be slightly loose. Sure enough it was! Another molehill I had once again turned into a mountain.

The Lesson

When we assume the worst, we seldom react calmly. More often we react dramatically and hysterically. When we panic, our minds become confused and we cannot think things through. It's a well-known fact that 90 percent of what we worry about never happens! Worry shows a lack of faith. Once you recognize this, you can make a choice as to whether you want to continue to live your life in a state of worry, confusion and reaction, or in a state of calm, trusting that things will work out. Then you can think clearly and take actions that will support you to resolve whatever is going on. This may mean letting go of the situation until it gets resolved. When you relax, others will relax around you. The solution will come more readily and harmony will follow.

Applying the Lesson

1a. Briefly describe two memories you have of making a mountain out of a molehill.

_____

_____

_____

_____

b. Is this a pattern for you? (Do you do this repeatedly?)

Yes _____ No _____

c. Is there anyone in your family who also does this?

Yes _____ No _____

2. What messages did you receive in growing up regarding worry vs. faith?

_____

_____

_____

_____

3. What is a more effective way you could deal with those times that you assume the worst?

_____

_____

_____

_____

4. The next time you assume the worst, summarize what happened in a notebook. Refer to this notebook regularly. You could title your notebook, "Having Faith vs. Assuming the Worst" or "Real Mountains vs. Just Molehills." Bit by bit, your behavior will change—or at least your reaction time will shorten.

5. If you lack faith about a difficult situation, prayer can help to bring you some peace of mind. Be open to adding your name to a prayer chain, or asking a friend to do a prayer for you. Make a choice every day to have peace of mind and a positive mental attitude. This alone can be of tremendous value.

6a. Go to the library and read the children's book entitled, *Chicken Little*. This is a story about a chicken who was frightened that the sky was falling.

b. Write any lessons you learned from it. Describe how you can apply these lessons to your life.

_____

_____

_____

_____

The strong, calm man is
always loved and revered.

He is like a shade-giving tree
in a thirsty land,
or a sheltering rock
in a storm.

—James Allen (1864-1912)
English Writer

The Airport Saga

Flying to Colorado for the first time excited me! I arrived at the San Diego airport at 6 a.m., tickets in hand. My reservations had been booked two months earlier, and I was looking forward to participating in a five-day workshop entitled, *The Magic Flute* (an opera by Mozart). Having enjoyed playing and teaching Mozart's piano music for many years, I knew that this workshop was going to be deeply enriching and life-changing. It was being led by Don Campbell, author of *The Mozart Effect*. Five days would be spent at a beautiful ranch in Loveland, Colorado, learning about and experiencing the healing power of music, as well as the healing power of my own voice.

I stood in a long line at the gate, waiting to get my boarding pass. At the counter, a smiling airline representative told me I needed to sit down. She promised to call my name after everyone received their preassigned seats. However, she confirmed that I had no preassigned seat. Completely shocked, I told her I had purchased my tickets well over two months before and that my travel agent had always booked preassigned seats for me. Her response was that the airline was waiting for volunteers to turn in their tickets and take the next flight that left two hours later. The representative asked me if I would like to take the next flight and receive $200. I let her know that my intention was to be on the original flight. (I didn't want to be late for the workshop.) I sat down and waited. I remained calm. Something told me it would all work out.

Fifteen minutes remained before departure. I realized I would be either on this earlier flight, or I would be on the later flight. Surrendering to whatever was going to happen, I waited patiently as the two airline attendants assigned seats to the remaining passengers. Finally I decided to stand behind the last two people in line and not wait to be called. Just as I got into line, a businessman walked up behind me. Curiosity made me ask him if he had a preassigned seat. He said he did not. My enthusiasm about the workshop burst out. I told him that the airline had overbooked and they were hoping for a few more people to give up their seats. He thanked me for informing him, and walked over to the other attendant assigning seats.

Five minutes remained before take-off. Then four words rang out: "No more seats left." My heart sank. The businessman overheard that I hadn't been given a seat and generously offered to give me the seat he had just been assigned. He told me he was willing to take the later flight. There wasn't a second to spare. I graciously accepted and thanked him profusely for his kindness. As I hurried down the ramp to the plane, I bubbled over with joy and gratitude. Once I settled into my seat, I looked out the window and praised God. How blessed I felt that there were such kind people in the world.

The Lesson

This scenario would have been quite different in the past. Instead of feeling calm, I would have expressed anger at being treated unfairly. Most likely, the consequence of my intense emotional state would have cost me the offer of a seat on the plane. It is clear to me that anger does not lend itself to others doing kind and generous acts. What works best is to have a clear intention of what you want to have happen and at the same time be willing for things to turn out whatever way they do. When you let go, an opportunity may present itself that you would never have been able to figure out ahead of time. Surrender and trust lead to inner peace, a calm attitude, and a higher likelihood of creating the results you want.

Applying the Lesson

1a. Describe a situation in which you got angry and you ended up not getting what you wanted.

_____

_____

_____

_____

_____

_____

_____

_____

b. Describe another way you could have dealt with this situation, which might have produced a higher likelihood of your attaining what you were after.

_____

_____

_____

_____

_____

2a. Describe a situation in which you remained calm, in spite of
upsetting circumstances.

_____

_____

_____

_____

_____

_____

_____

_____

b. What resulted? _____

_____

_____

_____

_____

_____

Every adversity,
every failure,
and every heartache
carries with it the seed of an equivalent
or greater benefit.

—W. Clement Stone
Author

The Teacup Story

Inspired by Reverend Joyce Meyer

There once was a beautiful teacup on a shelf. A couple came into a store and commented on how very beautiful it was. Suddenly the teacup responded:

I haven't always been this way. Let me tell you my story. At first I was a lump of clay. Someone beat me and pinched me (that hurt), and then they slapped me around on a board. As if that wasn't enough, they spun me around and around and around, and kept pinching me and changing my shape. It was awful! Then they painted me and stuck me in an oven. Wow, was it ever warm in there! There was a small window in the oven and someone kept peeking in to see how I was. I thought, Don't you love me? Why are you doing this to me? Then they took me out and put more goop on me and put me back in the oven, where it was seven times hotter. I just couldn't believe it! I thought it would never end. By that time I was sure no one loved me. Finally, they took me out and set me on a shelf. Several people came by and said how beautiful I was. The shelf had a mirror on it and I happened to catch a glimpse of myself for the first time.

I was amazed! I was really as beautiful as they said. I would never have expected that my life would turn out this way.

The Lesson

Do not always judge what is happening to you as bad. You do not always know exactly what is going on (the bigger picture). Perhaps results of actions you took previously have not fully shown up yet. We often get frustrated because we think things should fit our own time schedule. We tend to get impatient with ourselves, others, and with God. We have all heard the saying, "Patience is a virtue." When we are patient, we often receive blessings. When we give up too soon because we judge something as bad, we often lose what blessings may be on their way.

Applying the Lesson

1a. Do you tend to jump to the conclusion that something painful that happens to you, like a rejection, getting laid off or fired, is bad?

Yes _____ No _____

b. Have you ever had a "bad" situation turn into a good one?

Yes _____ No _____

c. Describe one or two of these blessings in disguise.

_____

_____

_____

_____

_____

_____

2a. Do you agree that patience is a virtue?

   Yes _____ No _____

 b. Would you consider yourself a patient person?

   Yes _____ No _____

 c. Name someone you know who is a patient person.

   _____

 d. Find some time soon to ask that person how they got to be so patient. Ask if she has any suggestions for you that could help you increase your ability to be patient. A telephone call or visit with her could be well worth it.

 e. Suggestions given to me and/or ideas I have for increasing my ability to be patient:

   _____

   _____

   _____

   _____

   _____

When you are pushed,
pull.

When you are pulled,
push.

Find the natural course
and bend with it,
then you join with
nature's power.

—Dan Millman
Author, *Living on Purpose*,
The Way of the Peaceful Warrior

The Faithful Farmer

Faith is the bird that feels the light when the dawn is
still dark.

—Rabindranath Tagore

I recently read a book called *Apples of Gold*, compiled by Jo
Petty. The following excerpt from this book is my favorite:

Faith is a gift of God. It is not a material that can be seen,
heard, smelled, tasted, or touched, but is as real as any
thing that can be perceived with these senses.
One can be aware of
Faith as easily as one can be aware of earth.
Faith is as certain as the existence of water.
Faith is as sure as the taste of an apple, the
fragrance of a rose, the sound of thunder,
the sight of the sun, the feel of a loving touch.
Hope is a wish, a longing for something not now possessed,
but with the expectation of getting it.
Faith adds surety to the expectation of hope.

I never really knew what it meant to live my life on faith until
I was forty-seven years old. Much of my learning came when my
husband almost died of a heart attack. When we are in crisis

CAROL JOY GOLDSTEIN-HALL

situations where can we get peace of mind except from praying and asking for help? I decided to call my husband's church and ask the new minister if he would meet with me at the hospital. He had recently moved to San Diego to replace the last minister who had retired. I rarely had been involved in my husband's church since I was raised Jewish. However, I felt extremely fortunate that the new minister came into my life at this very critical time. He made a huge difference because he was truly there for me, praying with me daily while my husband was in Intensive Care. It was a frightening situation for me and prayer was the only thing that soothed me.

It is difficult to be thankful when situations are so bleak, and yet I have learned to find things to be thankful for, even in the worst of times. One of the scriptures that has continued to provide me with hope is Psalms 30:5 which says, "Weeping may endure for a night, but joy cometh in the morning." I believe that my husband Glen's deep faith was one of the factors that helped him to regain his health. Many people's prayers were another important factor. Through this episode and several others, I have learned that I am not alone. Even in the darkest of moments God is with me. "Faith is a gift of God," as it states in *Apples of Gold.* I understand this now.

There is a famous Taoist story about a farmer. The villagers came to his farm one day and said, "My! That's a great misfortune! Your son has broken his leg; now he can't help you in the fields." The farmer answered that it was neither a fortune nor a misfortune. A day later, the government troops came to the village looking for young men for the army. They had to leave the boy behind because his leg was broken. Some time later, the farmer's horse jumped the fence and ran away. The villagers came to him once again and told him what a great misfortune it was that his horse had run away. The farmer's attitude remained the same, repeating that it was neither a fortune nor a misfortune. Two or three days later, the horse returned with a dozen wild horses following behind. The villagers came to him once more and told him what a great

•154•

fortune it was that his horse came back with twelve others. He replied for the third time that it was neither a fortune nor a misfortune.

The Lesson

The farmer was open to what life brought him, rather than judging what happened to him. In this way, he didn't experience his life as a roller coaster. No matter what happened, his ride was smooth because of how he interpreted the events of his life. He was able to look at the bigger picture. He exemplified faith. Stuart Wilde explained that we should "remember the teachings of the Tao: nothing is long or short, hot or cold, good or bad. If you define it thus, you have to ask yourself, 'Good in relation to what? Bad in relation to what?' Once you accept and disengage, you're free, and that's important."

As we let go and have faith that we are in good hands (God's hands), we will be able to meet life's challenges with ease, much like the farmer in the story.

Applying the Lesson

1a. Do you identify more with the villagers or with the faithful farmer?

_____

b. Give an example from your life that demonstrates why you chose this answer.

_____

2a. Describe the last time you griped about an unfortunate situation that happened to you instead of thinking that it may have happened for the best.

_____

_____

_____

_____

b. What is one thing you learned from the situation you just described?

_____

_____

_____

_____

3a. In your childhood, were you taught how to live by faith?

Yes _____ No _____

b. If yes, who modeled this for you?

_____

c. If no, what message did you get from your parents instead? (For example, blame yourself, blame others, get angry and quit if the going gets rough, etc.)

_____

_____

_____

_____

d. Did you receive mixed messages from your parents or older family members about worry, doubt and fear versus trust and faith?

Yes _____ No _____

e. If so, give an example. _____

_____

_____

_____

_____

_____

4. "Do not worry about whether or not the sun will rise; be prepared to enjoy it."

—Apples of Gold

a. On a scale of one to ten, where would you place yourself as far as agreeing with the quotation written above?

1   2   3   4   5   6   7   8   9   10

b. What is something that you are worried about right now?

_____

_____

_____

_____

c. Rather than worrying about it, describe a few alternatives
    that would be more useful in creating the results you want.
    (For example, say a prayer, etc.)

    1. _____

    _____

    2. _____

    _____

    _____

    3. _____

    _____

    _____

d. Borrow a bible and read Matthew 6:25-34. An easy-to-read
    Bible with excellent footnotes is the *Life Application Bible.*

Worry vs. Faith

So I tell you, don't worry about everyday life—whether you have enough food, drink, and clothes. Doesn't life consist of more than food and clothing? Look at the birds. They don't need to plant or harvest or put food in barns because your heavenly Father feeds them. And you are far more valuable to Him than they are. Can all your worries add a single moment to your life? Of course not.
—Matthew 6:25

Fear vs. Trusting God

So don't worry about tomorrow, for tomorrow will bring its own worries. Today's trouble is enough for today. If you worry, your fear will make it difficult to trust God. Don't let your plans interfere with your relationship with God.
—Matthew 6:34

Treat people as if they were what they ought to be, and you help them to become what they are capable of being.

—Goethe
German Poet, Novelist, Playwright, Philosopher

She Who Weaves Rainbows

Success! One of my out of town clients called me to tell me that her two-day workshop had just completed. She had finally taken what she considered to be a calculated risk in her life. (By taking a risk, I mean going beyond her comfort zone.) I had recently consulted with her on producing her first workshop and supported her through her fears of rejection and failure. She happily confided that her confidence began to soar as each person decided to enroll.

During our phone conversation I acknowledged her for producing a successful workshop that positively impacted the health of several people. While I was speaking to her, I couldn't help but admire my favorite watercolor painting hanging on the wall across from me. It depicted a woman with beautifully-colored butterfly wings, freely flying towards the sun. The artist, Meredith Miller, named this painting, *She Who Weaves Rainbows*. Suddenly, I began to see that this painting was not only about freedom but about living one's full potential. Realizing this, I began to describe to my client what I saw as her full potential self. Her energy seemed to expand as if to fill the entire room. It felt as if she were literally huge. When she thanked me, I could feel her whole body smiling, even though she was one thousand miles away.

This painting has positively impacted and deeply touched

many of my clients and friends due to the overwhelming sense of freedom it embodies. I had longed to own some of Meredith Miller's paintings, but never thought I would be able to afford them. One day I visited her home when she was having an art auction and saw a painting I really liked. Something told me to return to her home later that day when the auction was almost completed. I arrived just as they were auctioning a different painting and I almost won the bid. Another woman, however, wanted it very badly and I decided to stop bidding and let her have it. It was a painting of a beautiful waterfall with what appeared to be two soul mates seated nearby. Since I had already met my soul mate, I believed that this painting had really been meant for her.

Only two paintings were left. I was exhilarated, but I wasn't sure why. When the last painting was displayed I became extremely emotional, and immediately knew I was supposed to buy it. It was titled, *She Who Weaves Rainbows*.

After a long bidding period between myself and another man, I won the bid. I was elated! The next day I asked the artist if she would take a few minutes to tape record an explanation of my new painting. Here's what she said:

> This painting is also called *Butterfly Lady*. You see the spirit of her own power now coming out of the cocoon of the past into the future of freedom, and her joy that she brings with her is seen through the colors of her heart. The gossamer layers of her soul are now peeled away so that this jewel that she is can be shared. She is here to unravel the web that has kept other angels of flight trapped [i.e., to help those who haven't as yet discovered they have freedom of choice]. She is here to free the heart of many and to be an example. So may this painting represent Carol's precious beautiful spirit, now available to fly and soar and be an example for all to now see their

own beauty through her eyes. This is my blessing and my knowing that this spirit, a mirrored reflection of itself going through the stages of magnificence, now is freed. And so be it.

Although I knew I did the right thing in buying this beautiful watercolor, I noticed I had some fear in telling my husband about it. He always preferred realistic paintings and the one I bought appeared to be more like a fantasy. Rather than bringing the painting inside my house, I decided to first talk to my husband about why I believed I needed to buy the painting. I was sure he was going to get angry at me, (a fear I used to have with my father). Instead, my husband understood how important it was for me to own *She Who Weaves Rainbows*. His first reaction upon seeing this watercolor, however, was, "You're not going to put it up on our family room wall are you?" I was able to respond with an emphatic and confident "Yes!" After he helped me hang the painting, he completely surprised me the next day by installing a spotlight for it. I was touched and felt unconditionally loved by this wonderful, unexpected gesture. *She Who Weaves Rainbows* or *Butterfly Lady* has not only brought me a lot of joy, but has impacted hundreds of friends and clients who have viewed it.

The Lesson

If something truly matters to you, take immediate action to go after it, no matter what someone else may think. Joyful surprises often follow that you would never expect. Trusting whatever signals you feel, hear, or see is the first step in learning to receive what you want. Practice saying "yes" to your desires and aspirations. Blessings will follow.

Applying the Lesson

1. In what ways do you feel free to live the life you choose?

   _____

   _____

   _____

2a. Name at least two ways that you have listened to your heart this past month.

   _____

   _____

   _____

   _____

   _____

b. What results followed? _____

   _____

   _____

   _____

   _____

c. Considering you had some positive results happen, do you want to listen to your heart on a regular basis?

Yes ——— No ———

d. *Suggestion:* It would be useful to start a journal, noting what results happen each time you follow your heart. Be sure to buy a journal you would enjoy writing in. Schedule a set time each day to write in it. Experiment for one week. At the end of the week, evaluate the best times for you to write. Taking your journal to your favorite coffee shop will make it something special to look forward to.

Each Day Is Like

a Work of Art

-Anonymous

Each day is like a work of art
That's yet to be designed.
An empty canvas waiting
For the dreams that fill your mind.

Your talents and your strengths
Are like the colors you can use
To paint the pictures of your life
In any way you choose.

They're sure to be original
And all the world will know
The inner personality
Your words and actions show.

So let the colors of your life
Each day create a new
And beautiful expression
Of the one and only you.

The Unexpected Gift

At the beginning of 1995 I met a young Somalian woman named Raho. She was one of my students at a community college where I had been teaching Intermediate English as a Second Language. On my daily break I always took walks with a few of my students at a nearby park. Raho was one of them. That's when we got to know each other more personally. I was extremely inspired by her positive attitude about life, given the enormous tragedy and difficulties she had encountered. At that time, I did not know the details of her escape from Somalia in 1992, but I did know that she had no idea if her husband was still alive. About six months after Raho's arrival in San Diego, the Red Cross wrote to her and told her some wonderful, long-awaited news. They had finally located her husband, but did not have a mailing address for him as yet.

A few weeks after hearing Raho's good news, I was given rather bad news. The college dean informed me that my fifteen-hour-a-week teaching position, benefits and all, would be terminated in two months. To make matters worse, there were no other openings available. I had been teaching there part-time for seven years, so this news came as a big shock. My love for teaching and my attachment to my students made it even more difficult. There were other teachers who had only been teaching there one to three years, yet were retained. How could this have happened?

It made no sense! It felt like someone had just removed the safety net from under me. Although I was quite upset, I knew there was some reason why this had occurred, but I didn't want to admit it. I withheld this disheartening news from my students until the end of the summer semester.

The day after being told that I was losing my teaching position, Raho came to my class and told me she had a gift for me. She opened a very large leather purse and pulled out a small ring. It was deep brown and looked like a wedding band. It felt like plastic. Raho explained that it was made from porcupine quills. She proceeded to take out a necklace that contained a number of medium-sized brown beads, also made from porcupine quills. Raho apologized that half of the necklace was unstrung and proceeded to pull out one bead at a time from her enormous purse. She explained that just before her escape from Somalia she had to take the necklace apart in order to fit it into another necklace made from animal skin. Raho did this so that she could hide the necklace made from porcupine quills inside the animal skin necklace, along with some gold and a few other precious things.

Raho had learned about making this necklace from an African tribe. She told me that they used to insert their valuables inside these animal skin necklaces whenever they were attacked by other tribes. This was to insure that their valuables wouldn't be stolen. At the time of Raho's escape, she put the animal skin necklace (with the valuables inside) around her five year old daughter's neck. She didn't want anyone to suspect it was of value for fear they would seize it. This necklace was the only thing she was able to bring with her on her family's grueling five-month trek to Kenya. Just hours before leaving Somalia, her nine year old daughter was taken by force from her home and mercilessly murdered. Sadly, there was no time to bury her or to grieve.

Upon leaving Somalia, Raho, who was two months pregnant at the time, frantically tried to locate her husband, who had escaped moments before the soldiers came for their daughter. She never found him. Courageously, she and her three children walked for three months straight, pulling her ailing father in a wheelbarrow. Unfortunately, he died along the way. It was literally a miracle that Raho and her family ever made it to Kenya.

Fortunately, the animal skin necklace around her daughter's neck went completely unnoticed. Once she and her children were safe, she was able to sell the gold she had hidden in the necklace and use the money for food, necessities, and her family's voyage to the United States. This entire experience led Raho back to God and to devoting herself to her faith, which she had previously rejected.

The timing of Raho's gifting me the porcupine necklace, ring, and earrings was uncanny. She had no idea that the day before she gave me these gifts, I had been notified that my job was going to end. When I understood that this jewelry was one of the only things she was able to bring with her on her escape, my heart was deeply touched. I felt honored that she chose to gift me something so precious to her.

The next day I slipped on the ring that Raho had given me. Wearing it made me feel like there was nothing for me to worry about. It wasn't that the ring was magic, but it made me remember Raho's plight, and helped me to put my situation into perspective. I began to believe that there was a larger plan at work in my life.

Although I had listened to only a small portion of Raho's story at the time, I realized that if this young woman could make it through a seemingly impossible, deeply heart-wrenching situation as she did, I could certainly deal with what now seemed like a rather minor challenge (losing my teaching position). I joyfully wore this ring for several weeks. Later, one of my clients was able to find someone to beautifully re-bead the porcupine[2] necklace for me. I began to wear it from time to time, with pride and deep humility.

The Lesson

Alexander Graham Bell once said, "When one door closes, another opens; but we often look so long and so regretfully upon the closed door that we do not see the one which has opened for us." How frequently this happens for many of us! We interpret the closed door as a rejection and feel pain because we take it so personally.

Understanding that the door has closed for a good reason allows us to recognize and accept new opportunities as they are presented. The next thing we know, we are joyously walking through that "open door" and experiencing the "closed door" as a true gift.

Applying the Lesson

1. Make a few copies of the quote by Alexander Graham Bell and post it in your office, on your telephone, or any place you are likely to notice it.

2a. Has a door of opportunity closed in your life?

Yes _____ No _____

 b. If yes, did you interpret it as a rejection or something bad?

Yes _____ No _____

Explain briefly _____

_____

_____

_____

_____

 c. Are you willing to see the closed door as a gift?

Yes _____ No _____

 d. If not, why not? _____

_____

_____

_____

_____

_____

_____

3a. On a scale of one to ten, how patient are you when you are waiting for a door to open (i.e., waiting for a good opportunity to be presented to you)? *Circle the number:*

(Very impatient) 1 2 3 4 5 6 7 8 9 10 *(Very patient)*

b. Are you content with your response? Yes _____ No _____

c. What could you do differently the next time that would make it easier for you to see the closed door as an opportunity?

_____

_____

_____

_____

_____

If you limit your choices
only to what seems possible or reasonable,
you disconnect yourself from what you truly want,
and all that is left is compromise.

—Robert Fritz
The Path of Least Resistance

A Twenty-Four Year

Dream Come True

Do you often feel like your life is so filled with urgent things to take care of that you don't seem to get around to creating the things that are really important to you? When we handle those urgent things, there is a sense of relief. Unfortunately, this relief is only temporary. Soon there are more bills to pay, emergencies to take care of, the car to fix, the kids to car pool, etc. There will always be expected and unexpected urgent needs— the problem is when we let these needs run our lives. Many of us believe there isn't enough time for us to do what is really important. Too often we put those things we deeply care about on the back burner and refer to them as the "someday I will get to it " list.

Wouldn't you agree that spending quality time with loved ones is important? In addition, the top priority for most everyone is having excellent physical, emotional, spiritual and mental well-being. Nonetheless, most people do not believe they can have this. A client once told me that she had to be sure her daughter had her needs met before she could take care of her own needs. I asked her how old her daughter was. To my surprise, she was twenty-six years old. My client had not yet learned to put herself first and trust that her daughter was capable of taking care of her own needs.

My high school dream was to tour France. I studied French for four years in Buffalo, New York, and was fortunate enough to have two high school French teachers who were born in Paris. They often showed us slides of their trips to France. I couldn't wait to tour many of the villages and cities I had learned about, as well as practice speaking French. I used to imagine myself flying to Paris, getting off the airplane, and immediately going to La Tour Eiffel (the Eiffel Tower). I would see myself standing at the top of the Eiffel Tower, joyfully viewing many of the beautiful sights (especially l'Arc de Triompe and le Boulevard Champs Elysees).

When I attended the State University of New York at Buffalo, I majored in French. I intended to visit France during the summer of my junior year, but instead got married. Unfortunately, I didn't believe that I could get married and also go to France. Two years later I gave birth to my daughter Nancy, and a year after that we moved to Texas. One year later my son Drew was born, and we decided to move back to Buffalo. There were always reasons why I didn't think I could travel to France (not enough money, having kids, moving, etc.). About eight years passed and I was sure we would finally go, but my former husband planned a nine-day tour of Iceland instead. Once again, I placed my dream on the back burner.

When we moved to San Diego in 1978, I recall telling someone about my passion to visit France. I explained that I was so adamant about fulfilling my dream that I practiced my French with a group of French women twice a week for seven years. In spite of my explanation, this person insisted I did not really want to go to France. Becoming very upset with his conclusion, I told him he was absolutely wrong. He argued that if I had really wanted to go, I would have gone by then. This discussion clarified for me that although my passion to visit France was still deep inside me, I had allowed a number of circumstances to stop me.

Years later I wrote down a list of things that made my heart sing. My favorite one was my longed-for trip to France. I promptly made the decision that no matter what my circumstances were at the moment, I was going to have tickets for a three-week trip to France and I would leave in five weeks. I had no idea how I would do this, but I was very excited about it. I asked a friend of mine to support me through any unforeseen circumstance that might come up. I was thankful she agreed because I lost my job a week later and almost canceled the trip. Within two weeks everything fell into place. Three weeks later I left filled with enthusiasm.

As soon as I arrived in Paris, the first place I went was the top of the Eiffel Tower. I couldn't stop smiling. I had finally created my dream! I stayed one week in Paris, followed by two weeks on a bus tour all around France, visiting thirty villages and cities. I spoke French almost the entire time. When I returned to the U.S. I was so joyful and full of energy about creating my dream trip that for a solid year people asked me what I had been doing. I know for sure that I would still be just talking about my dream if I had not made a choice to go to France "no matter what!"

The Lesson

We often have our rationalizations or excuses for why we don't have what we want in our lives. Many of us spend more time focusing on what we don't want than on what we do want. Whenever we decide on something that really matters to us and start taking action towards bringing it about, situations that look like obstacles often come up. It's essential to then focus on what you do want and make a solid choice to create it. Asking a friend to support you, no matter what, really works. The joy and satisfaction of the results that follow will forever inspire you.

Applying the Lesson

1a. One desire I have had since childhood or young adulthood
is: _____

_____

_____

_____

_____

b. Another desire that really matters to me is:

_____

_____

_____

_____

c. Some of the circumstances (time, money, approval from other
people, etc.) and beliefs that are stopping me from pursuing
these desires are:

_____

_____

_____

d. One person who I can ask to support and encourage me in making a commitment to creating these important desires is:

_____

e. By the following date: _____ I will ask this person to support me in taking three to five actions that could assist me in bringing about my desired result.

Examples of Actions:

- Call travel agent   • Look at cars

- Apply for a loan   • Join a health spa

- Cut out pictures of   • Choose date for
  dream home   weekend away

- Find a workout partner   • Buy art supplies

Before each action, write a date this action will be completed by:

Date: _____ Action: _____

_____

_____

Date: _____ Action: _____

_____

_____

Date: _____ Action: _____

_____

_____

Date: _____ Action: _____

_____

_____

Date: _____ Action: _____

_____

_____

If you follow your bliss you put yourself on a kind of track that has been there all the while, waiting for you, and the life that you ought to be living is the one you are living. When you can see that, you begin to meet people who are in your field of bliss, and they open the doors to you. I say follow your bliss and don't be afraid and doors will open where you didn't know they were going to be.

—Joseph Campbell
Author and Mythologist

Falling . . . But Not in Love

"I can't believe it! I can't believe it!" I shouted as I lay on the couch at church in excruciating pain. "Please don't let it be broken," I begged out loud. It was Sunday morning, and I had just finished accompanying my husband on the piano. He was practicing the tenor part for his first quintet singing performance, which was about to take place during the next church service. Everything had been going smoothly until I started to walk out of the room. People began talking to me. I was holding the music book in one hand and my purse in the other as I proceeded to step outside, oblivious to the one small step down. The heel of my shoe caught on the top of the stair and I gracefully came tumbling down onto the pavement. Unfortunately, the concrete did not soften under my right foot as I fell. There I lay, dressed in a beautiful, long, chiffon white skirt and a bright purple silk top. What a contrast to my face, which was wearing a grimace because the pain was so intense! Immediately four men carried me back into the room and laid me down on a couch. Someone went to get my husband while everyone else tried to calm me down. I kept crying and blaming myself for being so stupid as to fall again.

My last fall happened about eight months before when a small amount of water and a peanut was accidentally left on the floor of a grocery store. As I slowly made my way toward the apple pies,

I slipped on the water and peanut, landing very hard on the linoleum and severely injuring my knee and left hip. It took almost an hour for me to get up. After months of chiropractic treatments, my hip started improving. Oddly enough, it finally stopped hurting the day before my fall at the church. Perfect physical health at last—or so I had thought!

While I was sitting in the emergency room on that fateful Sunday morning, I wondered why all this was happening to me again. Only a few hours before I had felt in perfect health. Now I found myself holding two packets of ice on top of my very swollen right foot and ankle. There was a little boy next to me with a broken arm and others in the waiting room in severe pain. Since there was nothing I could do about my situation, I decided to breathe deeply and tried to relax. This was not an easy feat for me, since I always had to know "the why" of everything (like a five year old).

Almost four hours later, a doctor called my name and asked me to have a fourth X-ray taken to verify if my bone was chipped or not. I got the results. It was definitely a chipped bone. Fortunately I was given a removable cast. In addition to the comfort of being able to remove the cast every few hours, I would be able to have acupuncture treatments, which I believed would help me heal more quickly.

Exactly two days before my fall at the church, God brought into my life a sweet and very knowledgeable, as well as spiritual, Chinese acupuncturist. I believe that meeting her was no coincidence. The day after breaking my foot, I scheduled an appointment with her. After her treatment she told me to stop worrying so much, and then confidently shared with me that God was watching over me and I just needed to have more faith. I wondered how she knew.

At a later appointment she exclaimed in her broken English, "You are so lucky to be born in America!" Then she related a story from her youth. It took place in one of the outlying areas of Taiwan where she and her family lived without running water and without cars. She explained she had to walk a number of miles to get water and carry it back to her family. The Chinese women had to be strong because all the men, including the younger ones, worked in the city and couldn't be there to help them. When her sister was sick, she had to carry her on her back about one hour to reach the doctor. She felt more fortunate than some of her friends because they had to walk two or three hours to the doctor carrying their younger siblings on their backs.

Upon hearing this story I realized that she was absolutely right about my good fortune. Surely God had taken good care of me all of my life, and in spite of my falls, both physical as well as mental, I was a very blessed person. The hardships I suffered were minor next to many people's sufferings. My acupuncturist's story helped me to put things in proper perspective and stopped me from blaming myself for my misfortunes.

I soon began to reevaluate my fall at the church. The day before my fall I had decided to take the entire day off and completely nurture myself. In the morning I exercised and had a massage. In the afternoon I ate a healthy lunch at a restaurant, tried out an inversion machine and had a manicure and pedicure. (Inversion machines turn you upside down and help to counteract gravity, reducing physical pain and sometimes eliminating it.) In the evening I went to a wonderful movie with my husband. By that time I felt 100 percent physically, mentally, and spiritually healthy and balanced.

That same afternoon I picked up a brochure describing the inversion and other movement machines. Before going to sleep I thoroughly read this brochure. One of the words suddenly stood out. The word was "shankara," a Sanskrit word meaning, "the one who brings happiness, peace and well-being into manifestation." Immediately I went to my computer and typed in the following: "My stand is shankara for all" and signed it "Carol Joy." When I went to print this statement my computer froze. (I got a little nervous when this happened, thinking it might be a bad omen). However, after fifteen minutes I decided to try printing it once again and it printed successfully. I went to sleep feeling very content, without any premonition of the bad fall I would be taking the following morning.

The next night I called my son to tell him about my fall at the church. When I related to him that I had taken a stand for "shankara," he responded that it was obvious I wasn't ready to take a stand as yet for all people's well-being. He suggested I might need some consulting to see what beliefs I had that were in the way of my own well-being. I found this wisdom to be food for thought.

Falling, for me, started in 1990. At that time, I sprained a few fingers on both of my hands after falling over a large cable at an outdoor Christmas concert. Two years later I broke the tibia bone of my right leg after falling on a wet rock. (See "If Only I Would Have Listened.") Following this I hurt my heel after falling while dancing at a party. (See "Deepening My Faith.") The two falls I describe in this story occurred several years later.

It was obvious that falling was a pattern. Even as a child, I remember constantly having a black and blue knee. I knew I needed to follow my son's suggestion and call my friend for a consultation. I seriously wanted to get to the bottom of why I had experienced so many falls from 1990 to 1999. Just before making this call I wrote down the question, "What do I need to learn from this most recent fall at church?" Then I closed my eyes and waited for an answer. I heard these words, "Sit and tune into God. You will be surprised at what information you will receive. Your faith needs to go to the next level." As soon as I began the consultation, I shared these words with my friend, commenting that I had hardly spent any time sitting and tuning into God.

In just two hours my friend assisted me in discovering that I had a major belief I had never been aware of. The belief was: "I won't be loved if I am well." I realized that if this were true, there would be no motivation for me to be healthy. Perhaps I had been unconsciously making sure that others loved me, by doing something that would bring me sympathy or attention. It seemed that I had to be needy in some way. The reward would then be love. The night before falling at the church I believed I was in absolute perfect health. The very next morning I fell. It all seemed quite bizarre. Maybe I really did believe that I wouldn't be loved if I were perfectly well. This was a very disconcerting thought.

My mom had always been somewhat of a hypochondriac until later in life. Then, she really did have some major health problems. Could I have jumped to the conclusion that the only way to get positive attention (i.e., love) was to have physical or emotional problems? During my consultation my friend asked me why I thought others wouldn't love me if I were perfectly well. I answered that if I were perfectly well I would have to take care of myself. I was completely surprised by this answer. It just popped out of my mouth. Then I began to realize that my mom felt loved when she was needed. That meant either she was helping those in need (particularly me, my brother or my sister) or she was needing help. Therefore, I could easily have believed that you are loved if you are in need. In other words, if I were in perfect health no one would need to take care of me and, therefore, I wouldn't be loved.

I began to examine the irrational and unconscious belief I had: "If I took care of myself my mom would no longer be necessary and, consequently, her love would disappear." I realized that this was a fear I had, but not a reality. What was really true was that I could be well and take care of myself and my mom would still love me. I had never understood that before. I was afraid of losing my mom's love. Therefore I had to play out the role of her child, meaning showing her I needed her so she could help me with whatever problems I had. The truth was I always had her love.

The Lesson

The more aware and clear we are about our beliefs (especially the hidden, irrational ones), the more chance we have of examining them. Then we can learn what is causing us to take the actions we do, and can subsequently be free to take actions that will support us in creating the future we desire. Otherwise, it's like being blind and having to guess where we are going. When this happens, it is far more likely we will fall. Once we are on a path, searching for the truth and being responsible for our actions, we can more easily begin to experience the harmony and joy we long for and the balance so greatly needed in our lives.

Applying the Lesson

1a. Describe a time in your life when you had something very upsetting happen to you in the area of health. (This can include a fall or other type of accident.) Describe it briefly.

_____

_____

_____

_____

b. In looking back, what is something positive you experienced as a result of this incident and/or what lesson(s) did you learn from it? _____

_____

For example, I was too workaholic and needed to learn to rest and nurture myself or I always was too much of a caretaker and needed to learn to be taken care of and receive love.

2a. Are you aware of any beliefs you may have about health or illness that could hinder you in some way?

Yes _____ No _____

   b. If yes, describe your belief(s). _____

_____

_____

3. Write at least two actions you would consider taking that would contribute to your health and well-being.

Action 1 _____

_____

Action 2 _____

_____

4. *Suggestion*: Laughter helps to heal. When you've had a reversal rent some humorous movies, invite some friends over to visit, or have a game night. It won't take long for your spirits to be lifted.

We get so caught up in the flurry of our lives that we forget
the essential things about art
that the act of creating is
a healing gesture,
as sacred as prayer,
as essential to the spirit
as food is to the body.

—Jan Phillips
God is at Eye Level

Once Upon a Dream

Have you ever had the passion to paint a painting, write a book or screenplay, act in a play or movie, choreograph a dance routine, play a musical instrument, compose a musical score, or start your own business? How often have you stopped yourself from doing any of these things because you were convinced that doing so was impossible or you just didn't have what it took?

The following is a story about something very surprising that happened to me. What I learned from this special experience is that we often limit ourselves and don't really know what is possible in life.

At the age of nine I began studying piano and at seventeen started teaching others. Playing Chopin, Mozart, Beethoven, Grieg and Debussy was my passion, yet I had never entertained the idea of composing a piece because I believed that people who composed music all played by ear. I did not play by ear. Therefore, I concluded it was not possible for me to compose.

One day I had some deep emotions come up, so I sat at the piano and thought of playing one of my favorite Chopin waltzes. Instead of playing the waltz something completely different happened. To my surprise, I started to play a piece that was very beautiful, so I decided to write down the notes. After about an hour I was very excited to find that I had composed one full page of music. Playing it made me feel very peaceful inside.

At that time I was studying piano with a well-known concert pianist. At my next lesson I asked him to listen to that one page of music. He liked it and strongly encouraged me to compose some variations for it. At first I was a little apprehensive, since this was new to me. However, I surprised myself by composing six variations in about a week. Now I believed I could compose!

A few years later I was drawn to sit down at the piano and compose a second piece. Some painful emotions stirred inside me. They had to do with a lack of love I was feeling and a hope for the love I dreamed of having someday. Words began to flow through me. As soon as I heard each note in my mind I was immediately able to find the correct piano key. It was as if I could play by ear. I wrote down the theme and found myself sitting at the piano every day, composing more and more of the piece. After about three weeks it was complete. The feedback I got from people was very positive. Not only did they enjoy listening to my piece, but they were deeply touched. Their hearts opened and tears welled up as they remembered long-forgotten childhood dreams.

About five years later, my family and I moved from my hometown of Buffalo, New York, to San Diego, California. Within two years of moving I separated from my husband after a nineteen-year marriage. Around that time I picked up the last piece I had composed and began to expand it. The beginning and end of it remained the same, but I wrote a very dramatic middle part that seemed to fully express the freedom I experienced after my marriage ended. I later came to realize that the piece, which I named "Once Upon a Dream," was a musical prayer for the kind of loving relationship I deeply longed for.

My prayer was answered about five years later when I remet a very special, loving and caring man named Glen. Up until that time I did not think it was possible to have the kind of nurturing, supportive marriage that the two of us have created over the years. I am thankful for this precious gift of love that I only once dreamed about.

Carol and Glen

The Lesson

We often lack the confidence that we can create something important to us. One reason is that we believe we must have the skills and abilities beforehand. All we really need is the passion. Our capacity to create is limitless. We can learn skills and abilities along the way just as Van Gogh did. His vision inspired him to become an incredible artist. Although he lacked talent and skill as an artist, it's known that he had a vision for his art and learned whatever skills he needed along the way.

Once you tell yourself the truth about what is really important to you, it's easy to take your first step no matter how small. Rather than seeking other people's approval, pursue what you love. Before you know it, everything will fall into place and your confidence in creating results that matter will increase.

Applying the Lesson

1a. In what ways are you thinking small?

_____

_____

_____

_____

b. Name a time when you stopped yourself from doing something because you thought you weren't capable of doing it?

_____

_____

_____

2a. What have you put on the back burner that you wish you had more time for, more finances for, etc.?

_____

_____

_____

_____

b. Is this something that makes your heart sing (your passion)?

Yes _____ No _____

c. Name a step you can take towards making your heart sing.

_____

_____

_____

_____

_____

d. Name one or more people you would be willing to ask for support and encouragement.

_____

_____

_____

Stop chasing your blessings, start chasing God.
God will then chase you down with blessings.

—Joyce Meyers
Minister

Living Your Life

as a Blessing

Have you ever looked back on your life and discovered that some of the anguish and disappointments you experienced turned into blessings in disguise? If you had known ahead of time that they were going to turn out to be positive, perhaps you would have worried a lot less about your future.

I feel very blessed and grateful that my parents' attitude and approach to life was "Life is a blessing." The dictionary describes blessing as "anything contributing to happiness, well-being or prosperity," and it also describes it as "a special favor granted by God." We all too often take our blessings for granted and forget to be thankful on a daily basis. We want our problems solved immediately. Many of us have not learned to be patient. In this day and age of fast food and immediate gratification, we expect instant results. If we experience loss, pain, or upset, we forget about anything good in our lives. Whenever we are reminded that we don't really know how long we have to live, however, we begin to appreciate how precious life truly is. Unfortunately, this is often short-lived.

When I was forty-four years old I accidentally found my baby book. There was a very special note in it that my mom had written about me, only a few days after my birth. It said, "We are going to call her 'Joy' for short, because that is exactly what she is, and her eyes are bright and full of life and joy." After reading this, I decided to change my middle name "Joyce" to "Joy." I have always had a joyful outlook on life and have tried to find the best in every situation.

When I was growing up I heard someone describe the difference between an optimist and a pessimist. An optimist is someone who wakes up in the morning, opens the curtains, smiles and says, "Good morning, Lord!" A pessimist is someone who wakes up in the morning, pulls the covers over his head, and says, "Good Lord, morning!" Obviously, an optimist has the attitude that life, indeed, is a blessing. A pessimist, on the other hand, sees life in a negative light and feels like a victim who has little or no power to change his life.

Does this mean we experience joy and good things every moment, every day? In a book entitled *Day by Day:Reflections on the Themes of the Torah from Literature, Philosophy, and Religious Thought,* the author, Rabbi Chaim Stern, addressed this very question. He said,

> We can't ask for lives free of problems. We can't ask for God to make us and those we love immune to disease. We can't ask God to weave a magic spell around us so that bad things will happen only to other people, and never to us. But people who pray for courage, for strength to bear the unbearable, for the grace to remember what they have left instead of what they lost, very often find their prayers answered. They discover that they have more strength, more courage than they ever knew themselves to have. We cannot escape suffering, but we may find God in spite of it, and even within it.

In the footnotes for Psalms 16:9 from the *Life Application Bible* it states: "True joy is far deeper than happiness; we can feel joy in spite of our deepest troubles. Happiness is often a temporary emotion because it is based on external circumstances, but joy is lasting because it is based on God's presence within us." When we base our lives on love for God and what He stands for, we will find contentment, joy and peace.

The Lesson

At any given moment we have a choice—the choice to be an optimist or a pessimist. We also have the choice of living our lives as a burden (i.e., feeling powerless), or living our lives as a blessing by being true to ourselves (having our personal choices really matter) and basing our lives on love for God and what He stands for. Those who choose the latter know how to take responsibility, ask for guidance, listen for answers, focus on their blessings, and feel God's love and the love of others around them no matter what their circumstances. This leads to an optimistic, joyful attitude in life. This is truly living life as a blessing.

> Lord, you alone are my inheritance, my cup of blessing.
> —Psalms 16:5

Applying the Lesson

1. Name some actions you have taken in the past that have brought you joy.

_____

_____

_____

_____

_____

2. *You may want to tape record the following visualization before doing it:* Close your eyes, take a deep breath and relax. Imagine seeing two movie theaters in front of you. The title of the first movie is: "Your Life as a Blessing" (self-sufficient, powerful creator). The title of the second movie is: "Your Life as a Burden" (powerless victim). Decide which movie theater you wish to go into. Walk into the movie theater and watch your life unfold according to the movie. Stay there as long as you wish. If you decide to walk into the other theater, you may do that too. When finished, take a deep breath, relax your focus, and open your eyes.

a. What movie did you choose and why?

_____

_____

_____

_____

_____

b. Describe your experience of watching the movie(s) you picked.

_____

_____

_____

_____

c. Did you have any fear about entering one or both of the movie theaters?

Yes _____ No _____

d. What was your fear or concern? _____

_____

_____

_____

_____

e. Was the movie you watched similar in some way to your life now?

Yes _____ No _____

f. If yes, in what way(s) was it similar?

_____

_____

_____

_____

g. If no, in what way(s) was it different?

_____

_____

_____

_____

3a. Take a moment to decide if you want to make the following choices. If you do, write your name in the blank spaces.

I,_____, choose to focus on my blessings and be grateful for them.
(Your name)

I,_____, choose to be true to myself.
(Your name)

I,_____, choose to live my life as a blessing.
(Your name)

b. If you decided you wanted to make the above choices, put them in a place you will remember to read them (preferably once in the morning and once in the evening).

c. At the end of each day you may want to write down at least two things you are thankful for (perhaps in your daily schedule or in a journal).

d. Pay attention to how your life unfolds in the coming weeks, months and years.

4a. What are some ways you have suffered in your life?

_____

_____

_____

_____

_____

b. In what ways did this suffering build your character?

_____

_____

_____

_____

c. Can you see how this may have been a blessing in disguise?

Yes _____ No _____

(For example, if you divorced and later met the love of your life or if you lost your job and later found your dream job.)

d. If you answered "yes" to the above question, describe how the pain or suffering you endured became a blessing in disguise. _____

_____

_____

_____

_____

5a. Even life that is a life of blessings includes suffering. If you could have your life any way at all, what percentage of your time would be dedicated to creating things you want, and what percentage would be concerned with avoiding, denying or minimizing pain and loss?

_____% Time dedicated to creating things I want.

+_____% Time spent avoiding, denying or minimizing pain and loss.

  100 % Total time

b. Are you satisfied with your answer? Yes _____ No _____

c. If no, what would your ideal percentages be?

_____

_____

_____

6a. What are some actions you can take that would increase the time you presently dedicate to creating things you truly want?

_____

_____

_____

b. Name one or two actions you can take this month that would exemplify your being true to yourself.

_____

7a. How important is it for you to commune with God and walk a Godly path?

_____

_____

_____

b. If the above are important to you, what is your next step in making them happen?

_____

_____

_____

_____

8a. What are some ways your life is already a blessing?

_____

_____

_____

_____

_____

b. *Suggestion:* Say a prayer of thanks daily for your blessings.

Before the Clock

Strikes Twelve

—Anonymous

I woke up early today, excited over all I get to do before the clock strikes midnight. I have responsibilities to fulfill today. I am important. My job is to choose what kind of day I am going to have.

Today I can complain because the weather is rainy or I can be thankful that the grass is getting watered for free.

Today I can feel sad that I don't have more money or I can be glad that my finances encourage me to plan my purchases wisely and guide me away from waste.

Today I can grumble about my health or I can rejoice that I am alive.

Today I can lament over all that my parents didn't give me when I was growing up or I can feel grateful that they allowed me to be born.

Today I can cry because roses have thorns or I can celebrate that thorns have roses.

Today I can mourn my lack of friends or I can excitedly embark upon a quest to discover new relationships.

Today I can whine because I have to go to work or I can shout for joy because I have a job to do.

Today I can complain because I have to go to school or eagerly open my mind and fill it with rich new tidbits of knowledge.

Today I can murmur dejectedly because I have to do housework or I can feel honored because the Lord has provided shelter for my mind, body and soul.

Today stretches ahead of me, waiting to be shaped. And here I am, the sculptor who gets to do the shaping.

What today will be like is up to me. I get to choose what kind of day I will have!

Have a Great Day. Unless you have other plans.

Giving Kids Choices!

All of us have choices. I recall learning about a situation in which an eleven year old was permitted to choose what time she wanted to go to bed. She had always earned high grades in school, so her parents thought it would be fine to give her this choice. However, she began to go to bed later and later. Then, she became too tired to concentrate on her studies, got sick, and missed school. Her grades began to go down. The privilege of choosing her bedtime was then taken away. She soon realized she needed to go to bed earlier. Once her grades improved her parents gave her back this choice. What an excellent way to teach children to make wise choices. This child learned that making choices was a privilege she needed to earn.

In another situation, a client of mine complained about her constant frustration with her young daughter's resistance to doing household chores. After speaking with me, she realized she hadn't given her a choice. I suggested offering her a choice of three kitchen chores. When her daughter got to make her own choice, she became far more cooperative and actually enjoyed doing the chores she selected.

The Lesson

Choices! Choices! If we are not given the opportunity to make choices at an early age, we often find it difficult to trust our decisions, try new things, and learn from our mistakes. When children are given a chance to make their own choices they may make mistakes, but they will start making wiser choices as they grow older. This helps them develop trust in their own decision-making process. Self-reliance and self-confidence naturally follow.

In addition, it's useful to explain to children how and why you reach the decisions you make. Learning more about how decisions are made will help them make better ones in the future.

Applying the Lesson

1a. Have you ever gone to a restaurant and noticed it took you a long time to decide what to eat?

Yes _____ No _____

b. If yes, the next time you go try taking only thirty seconds to make a choice. Then close the menu and order. The worst thing that could happen is that you don't like what you ordered. This quick decision-making practice will help you to increase your ability to make choices you are satisfied with (and save you time).

2a. At what age did your parents start letting you make your own decisions about small things? _____ about big things? _____

b. Did they ever include you in family decisions?

Yes _____ No _____

c. How did you feel when that happened?

_____

_____

_____

d. How do you think this affected you later in life?

_____

_____

_____

_____

3. If you have children (or were to have children), how can you help them to become confident in their decision-making process? _____

_____

_____

_____

4. How can you increase your confidence in your own decision-making process?

_____

_____

_____

5a. Is there an important decision you need to make over the next six to twelve months?

Yes _____ No _____

b. If yes, what is the decision you must make?

_____

_____

_____

c. What are some things you can do to make this decision-making process easier for you?

_____

_____

_____

With kindness,
with love and compassion,
with this feeling that is the essence of brotherhood,
sisterhood,
one will have inner peace.
This compassionate feeling is the basis of inner peace.

—Dalai Lama

T.E.A.M.–

Together Everyone Achieves More

A group of nine physically—and mentally-challenged children were at the starting line of a Special Olympics race. All of them were excited about winning. The gun went off and they started running. Suddenly, a little boy stumbled and fell. The other children heard him crying and immediately turned around. Each one of them went back to help him. One little girl with Down Syndrome kissed his cheek and said, "That will make it feel better." Then they helped him up and all nine of them held hands. They kept on going until they crossed the finish line. The spectators stood up and applauded, tears streaming down many of their faces.[3]

The Lesson

Competition is often very motivating and most of us enjoy winning. When winning becomes more important than the well-being of others, however, we need to take notice of this and reevaluate our priorities. In other words, although winning may be important, we need to remember that we are all here to help each other.

That is really what winning is all about. T.E.A.M.–Together Everyone Achieves More.

Applying the Lesson

1a. Was there a time when winning became the be-all and end-all of your life?

Yes _____ No _____

b. If yes, how would you do it differently today?_____

_____

_____

_____

2. Think of a time when you won something or perhaps came very close to winning. Who helped support you to come that far? _____

_____

3a. Think of a time when you lost something and felt like a loser. Who believed in you and gave you encouragement to try again?

_____

b. Did you listen to her encouraging words and try again?

Yes _____ No _____

c. If yes, what resulted? _____

_____

_____

d. If no, what resulted? _____

_____

_____

4. When I taught English as a Second Language, I had a vocabulary game every Friday and split my class into two teams. I always reminded them that the word team stood for "Together Everyone Achieves More." One team became "the winners" and the other team "the learners."

a. When you make mistakes or don't succeed at something, remind yourself that you are a learner, not a loser.

b. Suggestion: Make a few signs to help you remember:

1. **T**ogether

   Everyone

   Achieves

   More

2. When I make mistakes, I'm a learner.

3. Life is about learning, learning, learning. That's the way the creative process works.

Nothing purchased can come close to the renewed
sense of gratitude for having family and friends.

—Courtland Milloy

Life as a Blessing—If Only . . .

Have you ever come close to losing someone you loved due to an accident, illness, or something similar? Before this type of trauma occurs, we don't always experience how precious this person is to us or tell them what a blessing it is to have them in our life. Even though we may deeply love this person, we too often take them for granted. Later we say to ourselves, "If only I would have acted more kindly toward them; if only I would have expressed my love more often; if only I had spent more quality time with them."

In the midst of a wonderful and romantic Christmas vacation trip, a nearly tragic bicycle accident almost took my husband's life. It was the last thing we expected to happen. It had been ages since we had ridden a bike. My husband had often spoken to me about his first job at eleven years old and how he had loved delivering newspapers on his bike. He was proud of the fact that he had never fallen off a bike before and had even raced bikes as a kid.

The resort we were staying at provided two free bikes for each unit, so we decided to take advantage of the opportunity. Every day we went out for a two-hour bike ride and thoroughly enjoyed it. Since we hadn't ridden in such a long time we never thought about renting a helmet, and the hotel had not suggested any nearby bike shops for that purpose.

The last day of our holiday (the day before Christmas) my husband noticed his front bicycle tire was going flat so we started back to the hotel office to have the maintenance people fix it. My husband rode over a speed bump and without any warning his front wheel slid over sideways, his glasses flew off, and his head smashed onto the concrete. I saw him hit the ground and lie unconscious. I was terrified! It took me a few seconds to remember how to stop my own bike due to the shock. Luckily a few maintenance people were outside with walkie-talkies. As soon as I yelled "emergency!" they came running over.

It felt like an eternity waiting for the paramedics to arrive. Until my husband regained consciousness (five hours later), I was unsure if he was going to survive. He lost his memory. He had no idea what had happened or who I was. His head was extremely swollen. He had obviously suffered a severe concussion. The paramedics were worried he had broken his neck so they laid him on a board and put a neck collar on as a precaution.

The first thing I did when I arrived at the hospital was call the prayer chain at our church. I had been a member of this prayer chain for almost four years, praying for hundreds of people. Knowing that at least thirty people were praying for him brought me inner strength and my faith increased. I still had no idea if he had broken his neck or if he would regain his memory, yet I felt stronger and more assured that my husband was going to be all right. (Only a couple of years before, I would have been hysterical for several hours.)

The emergency room was having its worst day of the year. The long wait was difficult for me. The nurses made sure my husband was resting comfortably, but they had to attend to at least three or four other major trauma cases first. Finally, after three and a half long hours, they took my husband for X-rays and tests. Two more hours passed. I was on pins and needles, but I kept praying and picturing everything turning out well. When they wheeled him back in my heart sang. His eyes were wide open and he recognized me. Thank God! He began to ask

me questions about how he got there. Then, when I asked him
some questions about our vacation, I realized his memory was
slowly coming back. My grin must have been a mile wide. A little
later a nurse came by and reported that he would be released in
about an hour. He had suffered a severe concussion, but nothing
was broken and all checked out okay. I could hardly believe my
ears! My prayers had been answered. What a blessing! It felt like
a miracle. Did you ever feel like you had a second chance? That's
what it was like. Nothing at that moment mattered except that my
husband was alive and was going to recover. He never
remembered what happened that day, but the rest of his memory
gradually came back.

This incident impacted me in many positive ways. Most
importantly, it confirmed for me how very precious and
irreplaceable my husband was. In addition, I became convinced
that prayer and faith are essential in any type of traumatic or life-
threatening situation. I am also grateful that little things don't
upset me as often now because I can see the bigger picture and
know what is really most important in life: good health, loving
relationships and God's abundant love, healing and grace.

The Lesson

The precious relationships we have with friends and family can
never be replaced. That's why it is extremely important to let
them know what a blessing they are to us on a daily basis. When
we think we have control over whether our loved ones will stay
with us forever, we set ourselves up for deep sorrow and grief.

We need to live life moment to moment and cherish our
relationships. In this way, life becomes more and more the gift it
was intended to be. Somehow in the darkest of moments, God
does provide. This doesn't mean that the needs you have will
always be answered in the way you expect and want. God will
bless you and be there for you when you live your life honestly,
with love and forgiveness, and with compassion in your heart.

Remember to take time to ask God for wisdom, guidance, and healing for yourself and the people you cherish. When you ask God to be with you in your heart and soul, you will experience what people describe as miracles.

Applying the Lesson

1a. Have you ever come close to losing someone you loved, or have you ever lost a loved one because of an accident, illness, or something similar?

Yes _____ No _____

b. If yes, did your attitude and/or behavior change in some way towards this person afterwards? Yes _____ No _____

c. If yes, describe how it changed. _____

_____

_____

_____

_____

2. If you have never had a loss or near loss of a loved one, what type of reaction do you think you might have if this happened to you? _____

_____

_____

_____

_____

_____

3. Do you believe doing prayer and/or asking others for prayer would strengthen and comfort you in this type of situation?

Yes _____ No _____

4a. When is the last time you wrote a list of the people you are thankful for?

_____

b. We usually express gratitude for our friends and family on Thanksgiving. Have you been taking these people for granted lately?

Yes _____ No _____

c. Write down at least *seven people you are grateful for:*

1. _____

2. _____

3. _____

4. _____

5. _____

6. _____

7. _____

5a. Do you have any regrets about your past or present relationships?

Yes_____ No_____

b. If yes, list them:

     If only I _____

     If only I _____

     If only I _____

     If only I _____

     If only I _____

c. The past is over. You used the best judgment you could have at the time. Why not make the choice to forgive yourself and let it go?

     I, _____, forgive myself for _____
       (your name)

_____

d. Is there anyone you would like to communicate with and/or forgive?

Yes _____ No _____

This communication can be done in person or in an unsent letter even if the person has already died. Keep in mind that forgiving another doesn't mean you are condoning their behavior.

e. *Names of people I wish to forgive*:

    1.   5.

    2.   6.

    3.   7.

    4.   8.

f. Which of the people listed in questions 5e. would you be willing to communicate with in person, or by letter within the next two or three weeks?

_____

_____

_____

_____

g. If you wish to communicate in person, is there someone you would like to have accompany you, to facilitate the communication?

Yes _____ No _____

h. If yes, when would you be willing to ask them to accompany you? _____

_____

_____

Prayer is not an old woman's idle amusement.
    Properly understood and applied it is
    the most potent instrument of action.

—Mahatma Gandhi

The Healing Power of Prayer

Prayer is an invitation to God to intervene in our lives, to let His Will prevail in our affairs; it is the opening of a window to Him in our Will, an effort to make Him the Lord of our Soul.

—Abraham J. Heschel

Prayer is spiritual communion with God. It is conversation voicing our daily needs, our joys, our sorrows—the things that shape our lives. Prayer is worship, praise and adoration, thanksgiving, confession and petition. Prayer is not only speaking to God, but also listening to hear what God has to say. Walter Wangerin, Jr., in his book, *Whole Prayer*, points out that whole prayer is a circle, closed and complete: We speak, God hears, God speaks, we listen.

—Brochure by the Women
of the Church of God
Anderson, Indiana

Why is it that many people pray as a last resort? They wait until the ship is sinking, so to speak, and then they pray for a miracle. It's unfortunate that it has to take a catastrophe before people make prayer a part of their lives.

When my mother was quite ill I sent her some prayers to read. Since she lived 3,000 miles away, I asked her if it would be all right if I prayed for her during our daily telephone conversations. I was often surprised at the words that spontaneously came through me. Many times my mother would cry during and after these prayers. She often teased me that I should have become a rabbi. I took this as a compliment. As a matter of fact, I performed a Jewish wedding once at the request of a very close girlfriend, and afterwards someone thought I was a rabbi. I believe it's because the prayers and Hebrew blessings I had given were spoken from my heart.

The following prayers are part of a collection I sent to my mom to inspire her and help her learn to pray on her own. She found them very soothing and healing.

> Give me strength to lift my spirit above the trivial,
> To bear lightly my joys and sorrows,
> And in love to surrender all my strength to your Will.

> —Rabindranath Tagore

Dear Great Physician,

We thank you for the gift of healing that lies within the body, for the person who has health, has hope, and the one who has hope has everything. Lord, teach us that true and total healing includes healing of the soul, of attitudes, and of relationships.

Lord, we may be whole in body but sick in soul and spirit. Help us to ask for your touch of healing to establish a right relationship with you, for from that source other healings flow.

We ask this in your name. Amen.

—Gerrit Schut
Prayers for Every Occasion

A month of praying on the phone with my mom seemed to speed up her recovery. According to her doctors she got well a lot sooner than they had expected. She entered the hospital with a critical case of pneumonia and was sent home with a clean bill of health.

The Lesson

Prayer can make an enormous difference in our lives because it's a time out we need in this very busy information age. It gives us a chance to say thank you for our blessings, to pray for others, to pray for inner strength, and to ask for guidance and wisdom. In this way we can restore ourselves and have a real sense of inner peace every day.

Prayer works. It helps us to let go of having things always be the way we demand them to be. It gives us hope in times of worry and fear. It brings peace to the saddened heart. It reminds us that we may not always know what's best for us, but we can ask for guidance in doing what's best (God's will). So often we only see a short distance ahead and cannot see the bigger picture. We don't know what the future holds. At those uncertain times, prayer connects us with God and reassures us we are not alone.

Applying the Lesson

1. On a scale of one to ten, how well do you cope in times of major stress or trauma?

   1   2   3   4   5   6   7   8   9   10

2. What are some of the things you do to calm yourself? (For example, call a friend, take a walk in nature, listen to music, go to a church or synagogue, pray, etc.)

_____

_____

_____

_____

3a. Take time each day to be still and praise God. Afterwards, write whatever you may hear your heart telling you.

Notes: _____

_____

_____

_____

_____

b. Be appreciative to God for all of your blessings, no matter how small, and make this appreciation a part of your daily prayers.

4. Go to a bookstore and look for an inspirational book of quotes, prayers, daily meditations, or anything that seems appealing to you that could be of spiritual support.

5. Read the Book of Psalms (in the Bible), especially Psalms 43, 69, 70, and 71.

6. Sometimes we think prayer should give us what we want. For example, we may think that if we pray enough then God will be our instant passport to riches. However, "we make plans and God laughs," as the little saying goes. Describe when you made plans and then God laughed, so to speak.

    _____

    _____

    _____

    _____

7. Matthew 21:22 says: "And whatever you ask for in prayer, with faith, you will receive." What has your experience been regarding this verse?

    _____

    _____

    _____

    _____

8a. When you have a heavy burden or feel very distraught, it is easier to have someone pray for you. You can call a friend or a minister, or ask to be put on a prayer chain. (If you don't want to reveal why you are requesting prayer, you can say it's a personal concern.) When a group of people are praying for you, you feel stronger. In addition, you will find tremendous peace and comfort when a friend prays with you and for you. It is a wonderful feeling to know that someone sincerely cares about you.

b. Reading a prayer can be consoling. However, it is deeply meaningful to go inside and pray from your heart with sincerity and purpose. You are speaking to God. Try speaking aloud in a soft voice rather than silently. Be sure to start your prayer with a praise to God for at least one blessing you have in your life.

Here is a prayer and an article for you to consider. (I sent these to my mom and they brought her comfort at a time of great need.)

A Jewish Night Prayer

Blessed art you Lord, God of all creation,
for you make the brands of sleep
to fall upon my eyes
and slumber on my eyelids.

May it be your will, O Lord my God
and God of my ancestors,
to allow me to lie down in peace and
to let me rise up again in peace.

Let not my thoughts trouble me,
nor fearful dreams,
but let my rest be perfect before you.

—Gerrit Schut
Prayers for Every Occasion

The Ability and Strength to Cope is Within Each of Us

—by Rabbi Jonathon A. Stein

Coping is just about the best that many people seem to be able to do when their lives have undergone a significant crisis or trauma. Whether it is death or illness, divorce or disappointment, each of us goes through periods when life challenges us to find a way just to put one foot in front of the other. There are, however, several paths which people may take to overcome the difficulties of life.

Some people rely on God and prayer. God can be a great source of listening, comfort and strength. Pouring out our hearts to God can unburden us and allow us to share our pain. Whether it is the ritualized prayer of the synagogue or the home, or our private meditations, relying on God and prayer is, for many people, the path which guides them along the way.

For others, it is the support of family and friends which allows them to keep going. Being a part of a community is crucial. Human beings who are isolated or alone have a much more difficult time in overcoming their burdens. Being able to rely on family and friends to help us physically and emotionally can be a lifeline at a time of crisis.

For still others, the mere passage of time can help to ease the burden. Time gives us a perspective; it allows us to see our problems in a larger context. Sometimes we simply need to take a deep breath and let a few days or weeks pass. Often things do not seem quite as bleak when we manage to survive the most difficult parts of our crisis. Although it does not make the pain go away, time is, indeed, a great healer.

God has implanted within each of us the strength and ability to cope with life's challenges, to do what must be done, to put one foot in front of the other. Each of us will find the resources in a different place, but they are there waiting for us when the moment of need arises.

The Chinese Song

I asked her to sing me a Chinese song
Her voice was soft and sweet.
It sounded like a lullaby
Children hear while they're falling asleep.

I imagined my mother singing to me
My eyes welled up with tears.
It brought back a childhood memory,
And calmed my hidden fears.

She told me to rest and be peaceful inside.
To let go and let things be.
I missed my mother; she left a year before
She passed away, you see.

How well we hide our grief and sadness
Numbing ourselves to forget,
And then the pain we do not feel
We only feel regret.

I've often read that music soothes all
So I asked for a Chinese song.
She sang soft and sweet, with a lilting beat,
Made me feel nothing could go wrong.

My soul felt soothed as I closed my eyes
In my mind I could hear my mother say,
"I love you, dear. God bless you. Don't fear
And all will turn out okay."

Yes, your loss may be great, and the pain too much
As you listen to this song.
But God is good, and when you look to Him
Your healing won't take long.

So be thankful for His gifts of friends and family,
Of life, of health, of joy and love,
And when you remember you are not alone,
Many blessings will surround you from above.

I asked her to sing me a Chinese song
Her voice was soft and sweet.
It sounded like a lullaby
Children hear while they're falling asleep.

The Healing Power of Music

The power of music to integrate and cure . . . is quite
fundamental. [It is the] profoundest non-chemical medi-
cation.

— Oliver Sacks, author of *Awakenings*

When I was in the middle of writing this book I asked a
special friend of mine, Paul Lloyd Warner, to collaborate
with me on the topic, "The Healing Power of Music." Since Paul
was a concert pianist as well as a music therapist, I expected him
to spend a few hours sharing his expertise with me. Instead, when
we got together, he began to compose some music for me on his
synthesizer. The next thing I knew I was listening to his lilting,
uplifting music. It was heavenly. Each note seemed to be filled
with God's love. It sounded like angels were plucking the strings
of a harp.

My eyes were closed as I continued to listen. Suddenly, I
began to think about the six-month-old baby I was asked to pray
for the day before. Although I had never met this baby or his
family, I imagined him being gently and lovingly rocked in God's
arms. I heard an internal voice saying, "He will be loved just as
baby Jesus was loved." The next thing I knew, the music
transported me to an operating room. I started to pray for this

baby and for all the surgeons who were going to be doing the operation. I could see the baby's heart and I trusted that all was going to be well. My hands were vibrating and full of energy. Then, I saw myself placing my hands on the baby's body, filling it with healing energy. I had never had such an experience before and it was so real and so profound that I started to cry. I picked up a pen and wrote a message that began flowing through my mind:

> Look into the eyes of your partner.
> What do you see?
> What do you feel?
> Touch their face—their cheek—lightly—their hair.
> Do you see their soul? Feel their spirit? Feel the love?
> Embrace them.
> Feel one with them. They are you–you are them.
> God loves you so much.
> Never forget that.
> Be thankful.

> You are so blessed
> Beautiful soul that you are.
> You can heal through your thoughts.
> You have healed many
> Blessed daughter, sister, mother.

> We have a rainbow for you.
> It is always around you,
> Swirling around you.
> We love you.
> Breathe, darling one, you angel!
> We will continue to bring you many angels,
> Thank you for letting go and letting God,
> Sweet spirit Carol Joy.

Receive,
No expectations,
Your life is unfolding as the music
Each day a new chapter.
Write—
Blessed One.

Within five days of having this powerful experience I had an appointment for a haircut. When I arrived a woman was almost finished having her hair done. Coincidentally, it was the baby's mother. My hair dresser was the one who had asked me to pray for this woman's baby. The baby's mother told me that the doctors could hardly believe how well her son was doing after his heart operation. She brought him home from the hospital in only two days, which was far more quickly than they had ever expected. She thanked me for my prayers and we cried together. What an inexplicable, yet blessed event!

This was only the beginning of many intuitive messages I received while listening to my friend's music. The next message I was inspired to write was called "The Voyage" (see end of this chapter). Within five days of writing it my friend asked me if I would read it during a piano concert at his church while he played the very music that inspired it. I accepted. This was my first experience performing in this way. Although I was nervous reading my poem in front of one hundred people, I thoroughly enjoyed it. After this event I started to compose many more poetic writings. I later came to understand that listening to music allowed me to quiet my mind. Only then could I hear, see, and write powerful healing messages and poems.

Within a few weeks my friend asked me to be a guest performer at his piano concert, to be held at a large restaurant. I almost said no, but something told me to accept his invitation. He asked me to perform the piano piece I had composed, called "Once Upon a Dream" (see story with the same title). On the night of the performance I pretended that only one person was in the audience, instead of the sixty who attended. This helped me to stay calm. I was then able to play my piece perfectly. Two months later I received the following letter from a woman named Terrie. It had no address, no last name and no telephone number. Someday, perhaps, our paths will cross again. Here is the letter:

Dear Carol,

My name is Terrie and I met you at a restaurant when we heard the beautiful piano concert. I'm writing to tell you that I loved hearing you play that night. It reminded me of my mom (even though you're much younger). Something about the way you played was filled with her essence. It was very special for me. A couple of days before the concert, I found out that my dad had cancer and I hadn't been able to get a hold of my mom, as she was on vacation. I can't exactly put it into words, but when you played, I was able to connect with my mom, dad and myself. I know that love is the great connector and can travel any distance.

So—thank you for bringing me a moment of peace with your beautiful music.

Love,
Terrie

This letter touched me so deeply I was moved to tears. I am so happy and grateful that Terrie took the time to write this to me and that she could find peace through my music.

The Lesson

Music can be healing to the mind, body and spirit, and can transport us beyond our present reality. It is important to take time to nurture ourselves with music that is soothing to our souls. Pleasant surprises often result, like the letter of gratitude I received from Terrie.

Applying the Lesson

1a. Describe a time in your life when music relaxed you.

_____

_____

_____

_____

b. What type of music was it?

_____

_____

c. Do you believe that music can be healing to the mind, body, and spirit?

Yes _____ No _____

2a. What is your favorite kind of music?

_____

_____

b. How do you feel when you listen to this type of music?

_____

_____

_____

3a. Have you ever had a healing experience with someone who used healing sounds or healing music, like a harp or zither (lap harp)?

Yes _____ No _____

b. If yes, what happened?

_____

_____

_____

_____

c. Do you know of anyone who has been healed in this way?

Yes _____ No _____

d. *Suggestion*: Find a store or go to www.angelharps.com and learn about the healing effects of harps, especially lap harps (also called zithers). Try playing this instrument with your fingers or a guitar pick. Try out different lap harps and choose one whose sound you prefer. Lay it over your heart and have someone play it so you can feel the healing vibrations. You don't need to know how to read notes in order to play this type of harp. Close your eyes while you listen to its soothing sounds.

4. *Suggestion:* Before someone has an operation it is extremely helpful to hear quieting music. If you, a member of your family, or a friend, needs an operation, bring a small battery-operated tape recorder and some calming music to the hospital. Be sure to play the music just before the operation.

5. *The Mozart Effect,* by Don Campbell, is a book that explains the healing power of music in depth. I recommend reading it if you have any interest in learning more about this subject. The subtitle is: *Tapping the Power of Music to Heal the Body, Strengthen the Mind, and Unlock the Creative Spirit.* The web site, www.mozarteffect.com, will supply you with further information and music tapes you can buy, even tapes for babies.

Dr. Larry Dossey is the author of *Healing Words* and *Prayer is Good Medicine.* He said, "Don Campbell may change forever the way we view music." Having taken Mr. Campbell's five day workshop, *The Healing Power of Music,* I completely agree.

The Voyage

Wandering, wandering,
I know not where I go.
      Led by a minstrel's music,
      Beating steadily and slow.

Why do I walk this pathway
Where many have walked before?
      Why do I walk this pathway
      And enter each new door?

I promised I would listen,
I'm learning how to be
      Please teach me Lord and Father
      I truly want to see.

I know so little about You
I haven't tried to learn
      I thought that doing was the way
      Please teach me to discern.

It's so hard not to worry
I wish I could be still
      I know it can be simple
      I want to do Your Will.

My love for You is great!
Please teach me to obey
       I pray it's not too late.
       Just help me find the way.

I honor and respect You
I promise to be still
       With love and caring in my heart
       My spirit You can fill.

Thank you for Your blessings.
Thank you for Your love,
       Thank you for my life,
       And all Your healing from above.

The 11:11 Painting

One day it occurred to me that something rather bizarre was taking place. I had no reasonable explanation for it. Whenever I looked at the time on my car clock or other clocks around my home, 80 percent of the time the clock would read 11:11 precisely at the moment I checked the time. I thought this unusual phenomenon was just a coincidence. However, what made it very strange to me was that I would jump for joy and my heart would sing as soon as I saw 11:11. I assumed it was just silly to get excited when I saw these numbers so I minimized the whole thing, even though it continued to happen regularly for several years.

One evening when I was attending a friend's birthday party, it happened once again. I looked at my watch to check the time and it was 11:11. At that moment, I had been talking with a few new acquaintances and couldn't help mentioning this phenomenon to them. To my pleasant surprise, one of them told me that he often felt just as excited as I did and had experienced this same phenomenon regularly. He recommended that I look for a book called 11:11 as well as a deck of 11:11 cards that explained more about it. I quickly purchased both of these items and glanced through them. My amazement increased as I read the little introductory booklet for the 11:11 cards written by Zera Starchild. I learned that this was not just my imagination playing tricks on me. In fact, there was something to it. By this time I was extremely curious.

The booklet stated that the purpose of the cards was to serve you by "reminding you that you are unlimited spirit, and helping you to live that unlimitedness more and more each day." The author described his own experience too, stating, "By embracing all of myself, including the dark that is within me which I define as my fears and unresolved issues, it has been easier for me to accept the totality of my being and the totality of the universe." Then he continued,

> Perhaps you are one of the many individuals who sees 11:11 frequently on clocks, signs or other numerical devices, or in dreams. It is like a cosmic wake-up call, allowing those of us who are ready, to begin remembering our vaster identities and our reason for being here at this time. What 11:11 offers now is the opportunity for us to begin living our wholeness. For many of us that means shedding false identities, shedding all illusions that the answers are outside of us. During this time of awakening you will remember many things that you have forgotten, including the tremendous power of creation you hold in your hands. This is the power to consciously create your reality as you desire it to be. All that is being asked of you is that your creations serve the One (God), for the power you have comes from the One. This is why it can never be taken away from you. Only you can give it away, and only you can take it back.

Reading these words inspired me to make a drawing representing 11:11 in some symbolic way. Although I had never considered myself an artist, I had taken two weekend art workshops a few months earlier. I enjoyed using pastel chalks and I still had a box of chalks and some drawing paper left. This made me decide to put up my easel and place a large piece of drawing paper on it. Immediately I knew that I wanted to draw a large tree, so I began to do so. After that I chose a bright red pastel chalk and made a large red arch over the tree. Then I made the red color from the arch flow through the tree and into the ground. Next I drew a flowing river beside the tree. On the bottom left side of my drawing I drew the numbers 11:11, also in bright red, followed by the words, "Activation of Angelic Presence" (these words were on one of the 11:11 cards). I was pleasantly surprised by the result.

I looked forward to showing this drawing to the creative writing coach who had been assisting me with my book. He was the person who had originally inspired me to do artwork that represented the overall concepts of my book. At our next appointment I eagerly showed him my 11:11 art piece. From the top of the drawing I had decided to hang a small, thin, round Lucite disk with a colorful wire angel embedded inside. He told me that he found my picture quite fascinating and suggested I do something I had never done before. By this point I trusted his judgment, so I agreed to try it.

First, he asked me to close my eyes and imagine that I was the tree in my picture. In other words, I was supposed to feel like I had actually become the tree. After I did this, he had me imagine myself as the river. Then he asked me to describe how I felt and what I saw. What a unique experience! I will never forget what happened when he asked me to imagine myself as the bright red arch flowing over the tree. My arms extended outwards, and suddenly I felt a lot of warmth and energy in my hands and arms. With my eyes still closed, I clearly saw the earth below me as if I were in a spaceship looking down on it.

While this was happening I began to pray for several people, mentioning each one by name. I could see the bright red energy flowing out of my arms and onto the globe below me. I asked my coach if he would like me to pray for someone. He requested that I say a special prayer for a close relative of his who was living in a distant country. She had been in a mental institution for many years. I pictured lots of red healing energy flowing into her mind, body and spirit, and I prayed that God would bless her and bring healing to her, if it was in His divine plan.

The next morning my coach called me. He was filled with deep emotion as well as gratefulness. He related to me that his relative had just called him and told him that she had been released that very morning from the mental hospital and sent home. I could hardly fathom this miracle that had taken place and felt very happy for my coach as well as for his relative. I began thinking that perhaps my art had an additional purpose beyond the one I had intended. It was at that moment that I knew it was very important for me to continue doing my art drawings, complete my book, and learn more about the healing power of prayer.

The Lesson

There are unexplainable events that occur in our lives. Instead of minimizing them, it may be important to take them seriously. One way that we can do this is by being open to new experiences and by learning more about those times when God answers our prayers.

Applying the Lesson

1a. Name at least one positive event that happened to you which you found to be unexplainable.

_____

_____

_____

_____

_____

b. Had you or anyone else spent time praying for this to happen?

Yes _____ No _____

c. Did this event deepen your faith in some way, or did you just think it was some coincidence or quirk, and gave the credit to "lady luck?"

_____

_____

_____

d. In looking back at this positive, yet unexplainable event, what lesson did you learn from it?

_____

_____

_____

e. Have you put this lesson into practice as yet?

Yes _____No _____

f. If not, are you willing to put it into practice now?

Yes _____ No _____

g. Name at least one action you could take this week to help you put the above lesson into practice. (For example, find a book that discusses the healing power of prayer and one that can deepen your understanding of answered prayer.)

_____

_____

_____

_____

_____

He who loses money,
        loses much.

He who loses a friend,
        loses much more.

He who loses faith,
        loses all.

—Eleanor Roosevelt

Deepening My Faith

One day I attended a friend's birthday party and danced one of my favorite Israeli dances, "the Hora." We were in a circle holding hands and kicking our feet up in the air when I suddenly lost my balance and fell. Not realizing I had twisted my foot, I got up and finished the dance. For a number of days I had difficulty walking on my left heel, but I just assumed it would get better. Instead, it got worse. For two months I couldn't bear to take even short walks. When I got up each morning I felt excruciating pain in my heel and had to walk on my toes. Finally, after about three months, I saw a chiropractor. He took X-rays and ruled out any major problems. My heel felt slightly better after each appointment, but it started hurting again within two hours. I became extremely impatient and frustrated by this.

One month later I met a sweet woman who taught yoga. After I spoke with her, I realized that she was right about one thing: my business had tripled in size and I wasn't really taking enough time to nurture myself. In addition, my husband, who was then my fiancé, had been working out of town for six months. His telephone calls and his flying into town every three weeks to visit me just wasn't enough to fully support me emotionally.

This same yoga instructor suggested that I start walking slowly through the house instead of running as if I were going to a fire. As soon as I began slowing down my pace, I noticed my speech also slowed down. Nonetheless, my heel continued hurting and I felt like giving up. I'm sure you can relate to situations in your life when no matter what actions you take, the result you wanted doesn't happen in the time expected. That's when you feel like giving up. I decided instead to be put on a prayer chain and have others pray for my healing.

Fortunately, a few months earlier I had made plans to attend a weekend convention for a health company called Sunrider International. I had been eating their special regenerative foods for many years and my body had regenerated to such an extent that my energy was always very high. Why on earth did my left heel still hurt?

The first day of the convention, when I entered one of the restrooms, I noticed a woman massaging another woman's shoulders. They both seemed knowledgeable, so I asked them if they would mind taking a look at my heel. I requested some recommendations for helping me to walk with ease. One of the women, named Susan, took one look at me and said, "Well, it's not your heel that's the difficulty, it's your colon." I was very surprised. She told me to start rubbing my stomach to relieve the pain in my heel. I couldn't understand the connection, but I followed her instructions anyway. After rubbing my stomach for five minutes she told me to try walking. To my astonishment, my heel didn't hurt and I was able to walk comfortably. Immediately I thought of the people praying for me, and that perhaps their prayers for me had finally been answered.

The following night at the convention, Susan and I ran into each other again. I agreed to do a brief consultation for her and she agreed to do one for me. I wanted to see if there were any beliefs I held that might cause my heel to hurt again. Susan directed me to lie down on an empty bench and close my eyes. She proceeded to guide me through a relaxation technique. I entered into a deep state of relaxation. Then, she asked me some questions about the pain in my heel, but my attention went to my stomach instead. I saw the pain in my stomach as a big black face that looked three feet wide and had a glum expression on it, like an upside down smile. Susan had me ask this black face what it was doing for me. It's hard for me to remember the answer because I was so deeply relaxed, but I do remember feeling that I was being punished for being a bad little girl. (I didn't play too much as a child because I feared something bad might happen to me, like being spanked or yelled at if I did something wrong. That's why I tried to be very, very careful to always do the "right" thing.) Next, Susan had me visualize the pain leaving. I remember sending it up to this beautiful bright light. It looked like a huge, brilliant diamond in the sky with a lot of light rays beaming down from it.

Suddenly I heard a male voice speaking a foreign language. Then, I heard Susan say to the man, "It's okay, I'm helping her to heal." The man said something else in a foreign language that I was unable to recognize, and I was so deep I couldn't open my eyes. Susan reassured me, saying, "Carol, this is a doctor. Don't worry, he's going to help you." I realized that this was not just my imagination; it was actually happening.

When he started to work on me it felt like I was having a chiropractic treatment combined with acupressure. I had no idea what was going on except that it felt safe for me to allow this man to work on me. There was no question he was a healer. At one point he helped me sit up. Then, to my surprise, he hit me very hard on my back at least four times and helped me lie down again. After what felt like a half an hour, someone helped me to sit up again. When I opened my eyes I saw a very nice-looking Korean man in his forties, as well as another man surrounded by four beautiful young Korean women in gorgeous ceremonial gowns. I was later told that they had encircled me, showering me with a lot of love while my healing was taking place.

When I got up I felt dizzy so I laid down again. The Korean man continued to work on me. When I finally got up, I noticed all the pain in my heel was gone. When I woke up the next morning, I was able to walk with ease. What an amazing and wonderful blessing to be able to have had this healing session from someone who couldn't even communicate in English. I know that it was not a coincidence that these people happened to come by while Susan was working on me. This event truly deepened my faith.

A very special blessing took me by surprise about one month later as I was typing this story. A very clear, loud voice said, "Your life needs to be completely aligned with God." I enthusiastically told these words to my fiancé, Glen. In addition, I explained to him that it felt like they were being spoken by God. Then I gave him my interpretation of this message. I said, "It must mean it's time for us to get married." Glen nonchalantly answered, "Okay." I was surprised and thrilled. Four months later we were married. (We were supposed to have been married several years earlier, but there had been many different circumstances and health challenges that had caused us to postpone our marriage.) I reminded myself, "God is good all the time and unexpected blessings can happen when you least expect them."

The Lesson

In order for healing to take place, a willingness to be healed is a necessary ingredient. In addition, it's important to take responsibility for your healing, whether physical, mental, emotional, or spiritual. Once you take actions, it is necessary to let go and not be attached to the outcome or to the timing. It's especially helpful to recognize and acknowledge that frustrating challenges have important lessons that accompany them—especially the lessons of patience and faith.

Applying the Lesson

1a. Briefly describe a situation in which you feel impatient or stuck. _____

_____

_____

_____

_____

_____

b. Have you stopped trusting (i.e., have you lost faith) that the answer will be there for you when you are ready or when God is ready?

Yes _____ No _____

2a. What lessons do you need to learn right now? (For example, patience and/or trust in God.)

_____

_____

_____

_____

b. What lesson have you learned in the past from a physically, mentally, emotionally or spiritually challenging situation?

_____

_____

_____

_____

3a. Describe a time in your life when you didn't get what you wanted, but later on you realized it turned out for the better. (For example, it was a blessing in disguise.)

_____

_____

_____

_____

b. Would you be willing to let go of your frustrating or stuck situation and say thank you for the blessings you have now?

Yes _____ No _____

4. Some of the things in my life I am presently blessed with are:

_____

_____

_____

Letting Go

Struggling to relax

Feelings of discomfort and confusion

Questions with no answers.

Where am I going?

What is God's purpose in my life?

How will I know?

Answers swirl around me

like autumn leaves.

Trust and believe

Listen and expect

The answer will arrive

Let go.

S. A. M. (Sending A Message)

I had always wanted a loving, nurturing, supportive relation-ship, but I doubted it would ever be possible. After separating from my husband, I flew cross country to visit my family in Florida. My cousin took me to a nightclub where she happened to meet a psychic astrologer. Although I did not believe in psychic phenomena, she insisted I talk to him. With only the knowledge of my birth date, he amazed me with his uncanny insights. Somehow he knew of my failing twenty year marriage and that it was in litigation. As soon as he reassured me I was doing the right thing, I had a feeling of inner peace. He confidently told me that I would meet someone special, my soul mate, approximately the same time my divorce became final. "I doubt it," I told him. He responded emphatically, "Don't doubt it!" I was quite surprised by his absolute certainty. I thanked him but gave our meeting no further thought.

Two years later I volunteered to assist at a personal growth workshop. In a large room filled with over six hundred people, I "coincidentally" ran into Glen, the general contractor who had remodeled my home five years earlier. After greeting him with a big hug, he mentioned how I radiated with joy and happiness. He suggested that I change my name to "Joy" because I was so different from the Carol he had known before. (Little did he realize "Joy" was my middle name.) Glen attended that evening because he had recently been hurt in a relationship and swore he would never love again. He later acknowledged that because of my "new" self, he decided to enroll in the weekend workshop, and left that evening with a ray of hope.

When I drove him home from the workshop a month later, he surprised me by tenderly kissing me good night. "You'd better not do that," I warned him with a slight grin. "I might get used to it!" His kiss made me tingle all over. This really surprised me because he didn't fit my picture of "Mr. Right." (Someone my age or younger.) Even though he looked and acted quite young, he was actually twenty years my senior.

After that incident, Glen telephoned me about once a month. When he found out I was a workshop volunteer and wasn't paid, our friendship blossomed. He realized I truly cared about him. Occasionally he asked me and my children out to dinner, but I never accepted. I preferred to keep our relationship strictly platonic.

Five months later, when my backyard fence fell down, I called Glen (remember, he was a general contractor) to repair it. I took him completely by surprise when I asked him for a kiss. (The second kiss was just as wonderful as the first.)

I then recalled two events which occurred almost simultaneously before our second kiss. The first occurrence began as a mistaken identity. I kept getting phone calls for someone who had the same name as me. For some reason, curiosity I guess, I wanted to meet this "other" Carol Goldstein. I was unsuccessful in finding Carol that day, but instantly hit it off over the phone with "the other Carol's" co-worker. She invited me to her home for a "table tipping" session. I had never done this before and had no idea what to expect.

Adele Tinning, a well-known author and psychic, who has since passed away, led this remarkable experience. I volunteered and was told to envision someone I loved who had died, but not to say who it was. I chose my father, who had died sixteen years earlier. Four of us sat around a table with our hands placed on the table top. As I thought about my father, the table started rocking back and forth several times. Each time the table tipped, Adele said the alphabet outloud: "A," "B," "C" . . . . When the table stopped rocking Adele was on the letter "S." I felt very nervous, yet excited. We started over, and the table stopped rocking this time at "A." After thirteen more tips, it stopped on "M." "SAM." My father's name!! I was instantly filled with emotion. At that moment, I silently asked my dad to help me find a supportive, loving, nurturing soul mate; one who would treasure and adore me. This entire encounter was completely beyond my comprehension.

If this experience wasn't startling enough, two weeks later, another mystical event occurred. A professional acquaintance who knew little about me, but had claimed to be very psychic, called me one day. He told me he was awakened at 4:30 a.m. with these big brown eyes staring at him. He only heard two words uttered, "Sam" and "commitment." "Carol, do you know what this means?" he asked. I nearly fainted. I was so shocked, I burst into tears. It was my father, "Sam." He had heard my prayers!

A month later, Glen asked if he could visit me one evening. I finally agreed. After listening to his adventuresome life stories, my heart told me he was "The One." I still had reservations, however, about our age difference.

Within a week, I received my final divorce papers. Suddenly, I remembered the psychic's prediction that I would meet my soul mate about the same time I received these papers. I was excited! Could Glen be this man? My intuition said, "YES!"

One year later, Glen confided that from the very first moment he laid eyes on me at the introductory evening, he knew I was the woman he wanted to marry. I then admitted I knew he was "The One" the very evening he had told me his life adventures.

Glen and I got married. Every day we thank God for the deep love we have for one another, and for all the seemingly miraculous "coincidences" that led to our meeting, remeeting, and marriage.

Speaking of coincidences, the woman who invited me to the table tipping session, psychologist and spiritual counselor, Dr. Masa Goetz, is the one who performed our wedding ceremony.

The Lesson

Our minds are often linear and quite analytical (i.e., rational). As a result we miss information that comes to us beyond our rational minds. In order for us to create, we must have a balance between using our rational mind and our intuitive mind. Tuning into our intuitive guidance (higher power, Holy Spirit, Creator, God) and then following this guidance, helps us to have increased trust and faith in the process of life itself. In addition, it provides us with an ability to create our lives way beyond what we could ever imagine possible.

Martin Buber, a famous philosopher said, "Stopping one's ears, so as not to hear the voice from above, is breaking the connection between existence and the meaning of existence." The power of this statement is clear. We need to remind ourselves of this daily. The following quote reinforces what Buber said: "Only in the silence of ourselves can we know what is right for us."

Applying the Lesson

1a. Have you ever had an unexplainable experience?

Yes _____ No _____

b. If so, describe briefly what happened.

_____

_____

_____

_____

_____

_____

2a. Is there something you have wished for, but have given up faith on? If yes, what is it?

_____

b. If this story has inspired you, perhaps you can put your wish back on your list. Describe what fears you may have of adding it back on your wish list (or explain why you have settled or perhaps given up on this wish).

_____

_____

_____

_____

3a. Get a blank sheet of paper and at the top write the following question: "What would help me feel at peace if I add my special wish back on my list?"

b. Read through the following exercise. (Taping it first before doing it would be quite helpful.) Be sure to have pen in hand before answering the question.

Exercise: Close your eyes, and with pen and paper in hand, take two slow deep breaths and relax. Imagine your favorite spot and see yourself relaxing there, feeling safe and protected. Now imagine a very wise person walking toward you, ready to answer whatever question you have. Feel warmth and openness toward this person. Ask this person your question, which is: "What would help me feel at peace if I add my special wish back on my list?" Then write whatever answer you hear, see, or feel without evaluating it.

_____

_____

_____

_____

_____

_____

c. After you finish writing your answer, read and evaluate it. If you believe your answer is good advice, make a choice to follow what your intuitive answer tells you and write the actions you choose to take below as well as in your calendar.

Actions I choose to take:

_____

_____

_____

_____

_____

_____

_____

4a. Write one more question you would like an answer to. (Not a "yes" or "no" question.) For example, what's the best way to _____? What's my next step in _____?

_____

_____

_____

_____

b. Follow the directions in 3b, but substitute your question for the one listed.

c. Write whatever answer you hear, see, or feel without evaluating it:

_____

_____

_____

_____

_____

d. After reading your answer, if you believe it is good advice, make a choice to follow what your intuitive answer tells you. Then write the actions you plan to take below, as well as in your calendar.

Actions I choose to take:

_____

_____

_____

_____

_____

_____

_____

The New Land

Entering a new land
Beyond thought
Beyond this dimension
Beyond . . . .

Moving quickly
Racing,
Racing,
Heralding in a new century.

A new beginning
Being in the moment
Done with the frenetic past
At last.

Ready for a playful, peaceful present
Filled with love, hope, faith, and serenity.

The Heavenly Bridge

In the midst of writing this book I invited a very special friend, Barbara, to my home. She and her brother, Daniel, also a dear friend of mine, had just spent Thanksgiving and Christmas vacation in San Diego because of a family reunion.

Barbara had been living on the beautiful island of Kauai, Hawaii, for a number of years. My husband and I were fortunate enough to spend our honeymoon there and found it to be a very spiritual place. Barbara revealed to us that a few years before moving to Kauai she had received a spiritual message that radically changed her life. This message directed her to move from San Diego to the Hawaiian Islands. It also directed her not to charge people for her consulting services. Instead, she was to live by faith and trust that God would take care of her. She knew this would not be an easy task. How would she survive? Yet, she was certain she needed to listen to this very strong message. Her first step was to plan her move to Hawaii where she used to live as a child. She did whatever it took to move there. Eventually she ended up on the island of Kauai.

Barbara became a model for me of someone who lived her life by faith. When she first arrived in Kauai and needed a place to live, she easily found a house-sitting position in a beautiful home overlooking the ocean. My husband and I were fortunate enough to visit her at this awesome two million dollar estate.

Later she committed herself to helping Kauai become a model community for peace and harmony. She videotaped interviews with key business and political people on the island, and had these tapes shown on television. In addition, her beautiful vision led her to put together world-wide conferences for women.

Needless to say, I trusted Barbara would be able to guide me to my next steps. Several years earlier she had coached me in clarifying a vision for my life, so when she came to visit this time, I asked her to consult with me once again. She happily agreed.

The night she came over, Barbara directed me to find three different-sized candles. She had me place them on the coffee table in front of me and light them. I followed her instructions and sat down on the couch next to her, paper and pen in hand. She told me to close my eyes, take three slow deep breaths and relax. Then she asked me to write down a few questions I wanted to know the answers to.

My first question was, "What will help me get through this transition time?" (I was referring to how I could go from "doing, doing, doing" to "being," namely being in the present moment and living by faith.) Words started pouring through my mind as soon as I asked myself that question, so I wrote them down as quickly as I heard them:

> Take your pastels and draw a bridge. The bridge goes into the unknown. There are pinks and blues and yellows, but you know not where it goes. Notice it is high up as in the heavens. It's a **heavenly bridge.** It's now time for you to ask for guidance instead of thinking you don't know, getting sick, getting scared, stopping, or giving up. Remember this: One moment at a time will lead you across this bridge. Tuning in and being quiet are very important. This is not wasting time. Please understand this.

My second question was, "How will I take care of myself?" The answer I received was:

> You will be carried across. Why do you think you must do it all by yourself? You have never been comfortable living in the unknown, but you will become more and more comfortable. The railings (on the bridge) are the invisible help that you will be getting. Be grateful and honor and acknowledge this help. Continue to write in your gratitude journal daily and be sure to be grateful to God always. Others will guide you and give you the information you will need to cross this bridge (i.e., to begin to live by faith). You will know who they are. You will need to take one full day off a week to go into nature and just be, read, and tune in.

Barbara then added, "The railings are the lifelines to the divine. Take care of yourself first before anyone else. Honor yourself on the bridge, as if you were God. To prepare to live in the spiritual paradigm, be in gratitude to God daily. Fast once a week. Pick the same day, and fast from noon to noon."

By this time, I was quite excited and pleasantly surprised by the answers I was receiving. I proceeded to ask a third and final question: "Why am I in this difficult financial situation?" The final answer I received was:

> We have been trying to get your attention by 11:11, but you have refused to listen. (See my story: *The 11:11 Painting*.) Stop that analytical mind stuff! Rest your mind. Be God's child. Enjoy music and being loved. Ask what God wants for you. Pray for protection and know that God wants to nourish your heart and soul. Tune into God's love, be lifted up and experience peace and harmony.

Barbara added, "All there is, is love. Love is patience, humility, joy, grace, truth and harmony."

About a month later I decided to draw the "Heavenly Bridge" as it was described to me. I set up my wooden easel with a large sketch pad on it and then selected the pastel chalks I wanted to use. Although I had no idea how to draw a bridge or an angel, I trusted that somehow I would know just what to do. Faith was already working for me. I turned on some relaxing music and closed my eyes for a few minutes before making the drawing. After what seemed to be around thirty minutes, I had completed about half of the picture. I looked down at my watch and was amazed to find that I had actually spent nearly two and a half hours on it.

The next evening I went to exercise and returned home at about 11:30 p.m. I took a long look at my picture, "The Heavenly Bridge," and was compelled to complete it. After drawing the last ray of light around the twenty-fourth lamp along the bridge, I signed my name to the picture. At that very moment I was startled by the sound of my doorbell. I glanced at my watch and it read 1:30 a.m. I wondered who on earth could be ringing my doorbell in the middle of the night! My husband had also stayed up late and went to answer the door with me.

A meek female voice asked if she could come in. She sounded frightened, and identified herself as one of my old clients. I hadn't seen or heard from her in over three years. We opened the door and saw her shaking like a leaf. After inviting her in, we gave her a big hug and quickly sat her down. We asked her what was going on in her life and how she happened to decide to land on our doorstep. My husband examined her with a stethoscope he had on hand and discovered her heart was sometimes skipping a beat. We offered to take her to the hospital, but she wanted to wait for a little while to see how she felt. It seemed that she needed our company and a lot of compassion, warmth, and human touch. After an hour she settled down and felt a little better. She hated where she was living and was terrified of the drive-by shootings that had been occurring there. We invited her to stay overnight.

After accepting our offer, we insisted that she go to the hospital the next day to be checked over.

The following day she thanked us profusely. She went on to explain that she had stopped at our home because she had felt frantic about returning to her apartment after work. Suddenly she thought of us and was certain we were the kind of people who wouldn't be upset if she rang our doorbell in the middle of the night.

I personally believe that in some way my drawing may have led her to drive to our home. The theme of my drawing was "being," rather than "doing" all the time. My client had been worrying so much and doing so much because of her poor financial condition that she had been unable to experience any joy in her life. By spending time with us, she was able to reconnect with God (we prayed with her). Her faith was renewed and restored. One week later she telephoned us to report that she was given a clean bill of health by the hospital. Hallelujah!

The Lesson

What we need for our lives to go more smoothly is literally right before our eyes, if we would just ask God for the answers, listen, and then follow the guidance we receive.

Remembering you are not alone is key. Trusting and believing that things will work out, even if you do not know how, will not only bring ease to your mind, heart, and life, but can also bring you answers and ideas you would not have thought of previously.

It is important to decide if you really want to live your life by faith. Of course, you are free to live your life any way you choose. The alternative to a life of faith, however, is a life of worry, fear, and upset (which you are probably already familiar with). Living by faith is done just one day at a time. Once you have made a choice to start on this journey, it is very important to be grateful on a daily basis for whatever blessings you have been given and to remember to honor yourself and others.

Applying the Lesson

1. On a scale of one to ten, how would you rate yourself overall, as far as your ability to live by faith? Circle your answer:

    1   2   3   4   5   6   7   8   9   10

2. If you lived by faith to a far greater degree than you do right now, do you believe your life would be better or worse? _____ In what ways?

    _____

    _____

    _____

    _____

    _____

3a. Describe a specific situation in which you let go and lived by faith:

    _____

    _____

    _____

 b. What actually helped you to do this? _____

    _____

    _____

_____

_____

_____

c. If you did not have an answer for 3a, what do you think has stopped you from living by faith?

_____

_____

4. If you are in survival mode right now, what is an action you can take to move you into faith? (This may involve asking for prayer, support, etc.)

_____

_____

_____

_____

_____

5a. Name two questions you would like the answers to:

1. _____

2. _____

b. Write each of these questions at the top of a piece of paper. (one on one page and the other on the second page.)

c. Open a bible or other spiritual book to any page you are drawn to.

d. Read a quote or paragraph and see how it might apply to your first question. Write your insights under the first question you wrote down.

e. Repeat 5c and 5d for your second question and write down your insights under the second question.

6a. Memorize this Zen poem and ponder its meaning:

> Sitting quietly
> doing nothing,
> spring comes
> and the grass grows.

b. My reflections:

_____

_____

_____

_____

_____

_____

_____

_____

The breeze of His grace is always blowing.
You have only to raise your sails to catch it.

—Sri Ramakrishna
Hindu Religious Leader 1836-1886

Somewhere Over the Rainbow

Some of my favorite songs are *Somewhere Over the Rainbow*, *Zippity Doo Da*, *When You Wish Upon a Star* and *Moon River*. All of them talk about dreams, hope and faith. These melodies always uplift me and make me feel very positive and confident about my future. Smiling is all I can do when I hear them or sing them.

One evening, around 11 p.m., I was listening to a new CD. To my pleasant surprise the first song was *Somewhere Over the Rainbow*. The pianist played it so beautifully that I was inspired to call my son and play it on his voice mail without saying that it was me calling him. He used to do that to me from time to time. Within two seconds of my leaving this musical message, my phone rang. I had no idea who would be calling me at 11 p.m. I picked up the phone and heard an old friend's voice on the other end He wanted to talk to me about a major move he was contemplating that would dramatically change his life. Having lived in Israel for ten years, he was thinking about moving back to the U.S. in order to be closer to his aging parents. In addition, he wanted to find a new career that would give him the opportunity to contribute to the world on a global scale. I asked my friend whether he had prayed about this. His reply was that he had not even thought of asking God for an answer. I encouraged him to take the time to do this, reassuring him that the right answer would come. He thanked me and told me he would follow my suggestion. How curious that he would suddenly call me only seconds after playing *Somewhere Over the Rainbow,* a song of hope and a song about one's desire for a beautiful new life.

The Lesson

Often we ask other people for answers, thinking they know better than we do. We don't realize that if we really want to know what is best for us we need to tune into a channel that most of us do not take time to turn on. What channel is that? That is the channel that God speaks through. Some call it their intuition, their inner knowing, or the Holy Spirit. If you are open to listening to this voice, you will be able to hear answers that can be life-changing.

Applying the Lesson

The easiest way to get answers to your questions is to have a pen and paper in hand when you ask them. Rather than analyzing the answer or wondering if it's the right answer, it is best to just write down whatever words you hear. If you see a visual image, then write that down. If you get nothing, then write down you are getting nothing. Often new information comes to you once you do this. After you are done, read and evaluate the information to see if you want to follow the suggestions you received. Sometimes you will only hear a few words, but as you repeat this process over and over, further information will come through you. Don't be surprised if the information you receive comes in the form of a poem or a picture. Remember to save the answers you receive. Months later they may still be quite useful in helping you solve any problems you may have or in determining what steps you need to take to create a more joyful, satisfying future.

Draw near to God, and
He will draw near
to you.

—James 4:8

Searching for God

In Hebrew the word Boruch means "Blessed." Often it is used at the beginning of a prayer such as "Blessed art Thou O Lord, Our God." This reminds me of a Hasidic story from the 18th century about an orthodox rabbi named Rabbi Boruch. It is told that one day the rabbi's nephew was playing hide and seek with his friend. He went to hide and waited a very long time. Finally he came out from his hiding place and found that his friend was nowhere in sight. He went to his uncle, Rabbi Boruch, crying and heartbroken that his friend disappeared and wouldn't come and find him. Rabbi Boruch's eyes also welled up with tears and compassionately he said to him, "God also hides, but no one wants to find him."

The Lesson

Like the little boy who was heartbroken because his friend wouldn't come and find him, so God may feel when we go our merry way, forgetting about Him and His plan for us. We usually do this when things have been going our way for awhile. That's when we forget that God had something to do with our successes. Some people begin taking all the credit. Others become so consumed with their projects that they forget about helping their neighbors. Many stop praying or asking for guidance, thinking it's not necessary any longer. Lastly, there are those who begin to take their blessings for granted, rather than being thankful for them on a daily basis.

Applying the Lesson

1a. Have you actively pursued God in your life?

Yes _____ No _____

b. Are you willing to give God a chance and let His love in?

Yes _____ No _____

c. If not, what do you think is stopping you? _____

_____

_____

_____

2a. Is it difficult or embarrassing for you to ask for support or help?

Yes _____ No _____

b. Do you believe you need to be the "Lone Ranger?"

Yes_____ No _____

c. If so, why? _____

_____

_____

_____

_____

3. *Suggestion:* Every day set aside ten minutes of quiet time. Ask yourself what is really important to you. Take a few deep breaths and remind yourself that you are not alone. Ask for God's guidance, strength and direction. Enjoy this gift.

4. Name a few actions you can take this week to make God more a part of your life. For example, attend a religious service, read the Bible, spend time in nature, sing spiritual songs (with a friend or a choir), find a prayer partner.

a. _____

b. _____

c. _____

d. _____

My God, I have no idea where I am going.
I do not see the road ahead of me,
I cannot know for certain
where it will end . . .
but I will not fear,
for you are ever with me.

—Thomas Merton
20th Century Monk and Poet

About Those Reverses

"To walk with God we must make it a practice to talk to God . . . ." Tears welled up in my eyes as I read this statement written by Joni Eareckson Tada in her book entitled, *Seeking God.* Why was I getting so overwhelmed with emotion? Here I was writing a book on faith and having trouble completing it. For months I would tell people I just had two more chapters to write. Then something major would happen to distract me for several months. I had never realized that perhaps God was using reverses to get my attention.

Once again I read the words, "To walk with God we must make it a practice to talk with God . . . ." How often had I been doing this? Only when something frightening happened or when I experienced some type of accident or health challenge. I put God on the back burner as long as things were going well. Why? I was too busy for Him. I didn't believe I needed Him at the time.

A well-known Christian pianist named Gloria Gaither in her book, *Decisions*, wrote: "Prayer is meant to be a part of our lives like breathing and thinking and talking . . . It is an ongoing process, not just an occasional religious sounding speech we make to a nebulous divinity out there somewhere." I wanted to get this message into my cells so I would start acting on it once and for all! Maybe I needed to tattoo it onto my hand or brain. I continued asking myself why I hadn't yet chosen to talk to God regularly. Perhaps I still wanted to be in control. I didn't have enough trust to allow God to be in charge. If I let go and completely surrendered my life to God, it would be natural for me to regularly talk to Him, listen to Him, and follow the messages I received.

Faith! I still lacked the faith needed to do this. Suddenly, I had an important insight: I needed to make a choice to take the time to walk with God right then. I had been letting fear get in my way. "I choose to walk with God, and therefore talk to God regularly," I told myself. I truly wanted this! No longer was I going to give myself reasons and justifications for not talking to God. Only time would tell how sincere I was about this. My actions would reveal my commitment. I needed to remember Proverbs 16:9,[4] "We can make our plans, but the Lord determines our steps." This verse can be understood to mean that the final outcome of the plans we make is in God's hands. If this is true, you might ask yourself, "why make plans at all?" The footnotes in my Bible explain: "In doing God's will there must be partnership between our efforts and God's control . . . ." In other words, as you plan your life, ask for God's guidance and act accordingly.

The Lesson

Wisdom is a basic attitude that influences every aspect of our lives. It includes honoring and respecting God, living in awe of His power and obeying His word. According to the Bible, faith in God should be the controlling principle for our understanding of the world, our attitudes, and our actions. It's important to be reading His word (the Bible) if we are serious about living a life of faith. Then, as we learn to trust in God, we will gradually develop the wisdom we need to lead a joyous, healthy and peaceful life.

Applying the Lesson

1a. Have you ever made a choice to walk with God and therefore talk to God regularly?

Yes _____ No _____

b. If yes, what happened? _____

_____

_____

_____

c. If no, do you want to make that choice now?

Yes _____ No _____

2a. Briefly describe a specific project you are involved in right now.

_____

_____

b. What is your purpose in doing it? _____

_____

_____

_____

c. Do you believe that what you are doing is aligned with your ethical values?

Yes _____ No _____

3a. Do you know someone who you can use as a model to mentor you in your walk with God? Yes _____ No _____

b. If yes, who is that person? _____

_____

4. Before you put any plan into action it is helpful to ask yourself if your plan is in harmony with your values and God's truth. Then pray about it. The answer you need will be revealed to you. Trust the answer.

5. Imagine how your life would be different if you put God first in all areas of your life. Write some of your reflections below:

_____

_____

_____

_____

_____

_____

_____

The study of God's Word for the purpose of discovering God's will, is the secret discipline which has formed the greatest characters.

—James W. Alexander

Learning to Have Faith

in God's Laws

We are sure of this, that He will listen to us whenever we
ask Him for anything in line with His will.

—1 John 5:14

People often resist laws and rules. I knew a lawyer who never
went the speed limit. As a matter of fact, his wife told me he
loved to speed. Sometimes he drove 95 m.p.h. When he was a
child, his parents were very critical and quite strict. He believed
that his freedom was severely and unfairly restricted. Later on in
life he went to the opposite extreme by minimizing the need to
follow rules and then proceeded to break them. This was exhibited
by his out of control driving. There are other people who grow up
with little or no restrictions. Later, they too resist most rules or
regulations put upon them. These people think that when they
have to abide by the law their freedom is restricted so they rebel
like a teenager. Perhaps they haven't gotten past the teenage
years yet.

If we have the belief that laws and rules are bad in some way,
it could make it quite difficult for us to heed the laws and
commandments that are written in the Bible. These laws are God's

laws. They were written to help us make wise judgments and bring joy to our hearts and not to prevent us from having a joyful, peaceful life. Psalm 19:7-11 explains that God's laws are guidelines, rather than chains on our hands and feet.

One of the most powerful experiences in my spiritual development took place when I was a child. Every Saturday morning I sang in the choir at a synagogue. I distinctly remember the rabbi taking the holy Torah out of the ark and holding it up for the congregation to see. I had a perfect view of him because I was sitting up in a balcony. To this day, I can still hear his deep, booming voice reciting the following from Psalm 19:7-11:

> The law of the Lord is perfect, reviving the soul; the testimony of the Lord is sure, making wise the simple; the precepts of the Lord are right, rejoicing the heart; the commandment of the Lord is pure, enlightening the eyes; the fear of the Lord is clean, enduring forever; the judgments of the Lord are true, and righteous all together. It is a tree of life to them that lay hold of it, and all its paths are peace.

Being only a child at the time, I never fully understood those words, but they deeply touched my heart and soul. Each time the rabbi spoke those words, it felt like God himself was speaking. This made a profound and lasting impact on me. In studying this passage as an adult, I learned its full meaning. "Reviving the soul" meant bringing one back to the Lord. "The testimony of the Lord is sure, making wise the simple," meant that the law of the Lord gives practical guidance for life. Lastly, "The statutes of the Lord are right, rejoicing the heart," meant that the Lord encourages and inspires us through His laws.

Why is it that laws are looked at as rules by many people? They react angrily to them because they believe that following these laws or rules is the same as someone telling them what they must do or not do. As a child, a parent has to teach their children many things, such as not to go near a hot stove. When they command, "Don't touch the stove," it's to make sure their children don't get burned. The principle for this rule is, "You'll be safe if you don't touch a hot stove or flame." When you hear the principle behind this rule, it's easier to accept it because you understand the purpose of the rule. It's the same idea if you study God's laws and understand that His laws were given to help create a civilized, harmonious, peaceful world.

It has taken me many years to understand the true purpose of the Bible and what it means to live your life according to God's commandments. I certainly am far from perfect, but reading the Bible has greatly helped me to learn how to live by faith. In Matthew 17:20, Christ told His disciples, "For truly, I say to you, if you have faith as a grain of mustard seed, you will say to this mountain, 'Move from here to there,' and it will move; and nothing will be impossible to you." What this really means is that if you have a problem that seems as big and immovable as a mountain, don't look at the mountain, look instead to the one who can help you with the problem. In other words, look to the Lord to deepen your faith. In Matthew 21:22, it says, "And whatever you ask for in prayer with faith, you will receive." Of course this is not a guarantee that we can get anything we want just by asking. It's important to know that in order to have our prayers fulfilled, our requests must always be in harmony with God's principles. Then we need to let go and completely trust in God's plan for us.

The Lesson

When we are children, our parents have rules because they care about our well-being. They love us and want us to be safe and out of harm's way. Unfortunately there are some parents who do not take care of their children's well-being and abuse them instead, creating an unsafe environment. Adults brought up in this type of environment often find it difficult to develop trust and faith in those who do really care about them. This can transfer over to having little faith or trust that God's laws were truly intended for their well-being.

God gave us His laws and commandments to help us make wise choices, bring joy to our hearts, give us insights, warn us, reward us, and in general, give us a basis for living in harmony and peace with ourselves and others. It would certainly make good sense to learn more about God's commandments, including the principles behind them.

Applying the Lesson

1a. As you begin each day, ask that God's love guide what you say and how you think.

b. In what ways would your words, lifestyle and actions change if you asked God to guide you on a daily basis? (Take a guess.) _____

_____

_____

_____

_____

2a. Name some commandments, rules, and/or laws that you have resisted following. (An example might be do not gossip, lie, cheat or steal; do not exceed 65 m.p.h.; wear your seat belt, etc.) _____

_____

_____

_____

b. What would the principle or benefit be for this commandment, law or rule?

_____

_____

_____

_____

c. Do you have less resistance when you think of the principle, rather than the rule?

Yes _____ No _____

3a. As you look back at your childhood, do you think it would have been better if your parents had been stricter, more lenient, or stayed just the way they were?

Stricter _____
More lenient _____
Some other way _____
Exactly the way they were _____

b. Would it have helped if your parents had explained the principles behind their rules?

Yes _____ No _____

c. If you have children, are you (or were you) stricter, more lenient, or the same as your parents?

_____

Why? _____

_____

_____

d. What results did you notice from your actions? _____

_____

_____

_____

4a. Are you sincerely interested in learning more about God's commandments and His promises? Yes _____ No _____

b. If yes, list a few actions you could take that would support you in learning more about living a life that can bring you the peace, joy, health, and blessings that God has promised.

_____

_____

_____

_____

_____

_____

_____

And without faith it is impossible to please Him,
for whoever would draw near to God must believe
that He exists and that He rewards those who seek Him.
—Hebrews 11:6

Learning Faith

Intellectually I believed that God existed, but emotionally I had never really understood what it meant to have a personal relationship with God. My dad had been raised as an Orthodox Jew (very strict) and my mom had learned to celebrate the Jewish holidays, but had not had any formal training in Judaism. I remember growing up joyfully celebrating all the Jewish holidays with my family and relatives. My mom influenced my dad in joining a more modern temple (Reform) since she didn't know any Hebrew and preferred to go to services that were mostly in English.

One of my favorite memories is of my mom making a special Sabbath dinner every Friday evening. My sister, brother and I would dress up, excitedly anticipating her delicious, special meal. Before dinner she always recited a Hebrew blessing over the Sabbath candles and my dad sang a Hebrew prayer over the wine and challah (a special twisted bread for the Sabbath meal). Every week he would make up a different melody. I clearly remember how he sang completely from his heart and was always moved to tears. I believe this was my first real spiritual teaching. It deeply affected me because it was a touching experience beyond words and influenced me to sing in the Reform temple children's choir. I sang every Saturday morning at temple services from the age of nine to the age of thirteen. I loved it! Our choir director regularly took us to several Jewish old folks' homes to sing, especially during the holiday season. I often played piano and sang duets there with my best friend. This helped to form and deepen my spiritual life.

When I was thirteen there was a bible class I attended at my temple. I have a strong recollection of my teacher asking us to describe what God meant to us. One of my friends answered, "God dwells within me." This way of describing God was new to me and greatly impacted my thinking. I started to do silent prayers and felt God's presence much more intimately. The following year I became an assistant teacher for the fourth grade.

Many years later, I had a very unusual and meaningful experience that I have rarely spoken about. I was trying to find peace and heal from my recent divorce. Coincidentally, I ran into an old friend who was a massage therapist. She suggested I make an appointment with her. It seemed to be the right timing for me, given my situation.

While waiting for my appointment to begin, my friend opened with a special prayer. My eyes were closed at the time, but what I saw was very clear. Something began spinning on the ceiling of the room. I described it to my friend as a very large silver salt shaker, but as I continued to watch it, the spinning slowly stopped. I was taken by complete surprise as the salt shaker turned into what looked exactly like pictures I had seen of Christ. Suddenly, he became alive and stood next to me. I started to feel a little frightened because the experience was so real. He spoke to me and said the following words, "Don't be afraid, just because you're Jewish." I started to cry. I had never had an experience like this before, but I knew that I hadn't made it up. I later realized that this unforgettably powerful experience was a preparation for me in deepening my faith, and in opening my mind to the wisdom of other religions, especially the Christian faith.

The Lesson

Faith in the *American Heritage* dictionary is defined as: 1. A confident belief in the truth, value or trustworthiness of a person, idea or thing; 2. A belief that does not rest on logical proof or material evidence; 3. A belief and trust in God and in the doctrines expressed in the scriptures and other sacred works.

Many people are never really taught to live by faith. If our parents modeled it for us, we have a better chance of knowing deep inside that God is really there for us, guiding and protecting us no matter what sorrows we may experience. On the other hand, many of us end up on a spiritual journey, often due to tragedies, divorce or illness. As painful as our path in life may be, something stirs us to move to our next level. None of us wants to stay grief-stricken or in a downward spiral.

Fortunately, inexplicable things often happen along our path that give us hope. Sometimes they arrive in the form of a very supportive person. What's most important is to be open to these events and/or people, rather than rejecting them. In this way, we have a better chance of learning to live by faith (i.e., trust God).

Applying the Lesson

1a. Do you believe you have a personal relationship with God?

Yes _____ No _____

b. If yes, when did it begin? If not, why do you think you haven't developed one?

_____

_____

_____

2. Describe one or more experiences you had in growing up that may have contributed to your learning faith.

_____

_____

_____

_____

_____

3a. Are there any religious rituals you observed or followed as a child that are still meaningful to you? Yes _____ No _____

b. If yes, describe or name them. _____

_____

_____

_____

c. Have you continued to do them? Yes _____ No _____

4. If it has been awhile since you have felt touched spiritually, list some things you might do to get back to that feeling. (For example, go into nature, watch children joyfully play, go to a church or temple, be in silence for a while, etc.)

_____

_____

_____

_____

_____

_____

5a. Is there someone you know (a family member, co-worker or acquaintance) who has a close relationship with God?

Yes _____ No _____

b. If yes, ask to speak with them about how you could have a closer relationship with God.

c. Take their advice and try it out (be open to it).

6a. On a scale of one to ten, how much time have you put into building a relationship with God?

1   2   3   4   5   6   7   8   9   10

b. Name the next step you could take in that direction:

_____

_____

_____

_____

_____

My child, eat honey, for it is good,
and the honeycomb is sweet to the taste.
In the same way, wisdom is sweet to your soul.
If you find it, you will have a bright future,
and your hopes will not be cut short.

—Proverbs 24:13-14

Love as a Blessing

To love a person is to learn the song that is in their heart,
and to sing it to them when they have forgotten.

> —Thomas Chandler

Be humble and gentle. Be patient with each other, making
allowance for each other's faults because of your love.

> —Ephesians 4:12 TLB

Do we have to love ourselves in order to be loved? I don't believe that we do, even though so many books and people seem to support this view. My parents loved me, even though I did not have much confidence in myself; my former husband loved me, in his own way, even though I did not believe in myself all the time; and my kids loved me unconditionally, yet I was critical of myself because I was unable to set boundaries with my two children. This is because I was afraid they would not love me if I did.

We often try to get people we care about to stay around by treating them in a certain way. It took many workshop hours for me to recognize that this type of behavior was manipulative. It took a number of years for me to completely stop this destructive behavior and become true to myself. (See "Turning Point" story).

If you interviewed one hundred people, they would all have

a different meaning for love. I knew someone who believed that if his wife didn't have fruit in the house every day, she didn't love him. (His mom always had fruit in the house.) His wife didn't know that he had this belief until she ran out of frozen orange juice one day. Suddenly her husband went berserk. Everyone has their own interpretation of love.

Depending on our upbringing, we draw conclusions as to the meaning of love. It's very important to know what love means to you, and what it means to your spouse, family members, etc. Otherwise, there will be many unfulfilled expectations, misunderstandings and painful disappointments. People can easily misinterpret behavior and jump to the conclusion that they are unloved just because their spouse ran out of orange juice or didn't buy flowers for them.

In truth, love cannot be described. When people are unable to live harmoniously together, perhaps because of incompatibilities or opposite values, love may still remain between the two people. I personally experienced this after my divorce. After breaking up, what can people do with the love? Time is the only thing that can heal. We need to be patient.

One day, I opened my Bible to try to find a particular passage from Philippians, but instead, the page fell open to Corinthians. My eyes immediately focused on the word "love." I knew I should read that passage. It was Corinthians 13:2-3, and it said: "If I could speak in any language in heaven or on earth but didn't love others, I would only be making meaningless noise like a loud gong or a clanging cymbal . . . And if I had the gift of faith so that I could speak to a mountain and make it move, without love I would be no good to anybody." How clear and powerful these statements are!

Love is as important as water is to flowers. It has been proven that babies wither and die without it. The footnotes in Corinthians explained that it was impossible to have this love unless God helped us set aside our own natural desires so that we could love and not expect anything in return. This is unconditional love.

I believe that unconditional love includes supporting someone when they are being true to themselves (even though it may not be what you would choose to do), being honest with them, and being there for them with compassion and sensitivity. These are some of the qualities of a loyal, kind and loving friend. If we think of people as flowers that need to be watered and lovingly support and nurture them, they will grow and blossom. The love we give without expectation will begin to flow back into our lives. Our lives will then become a blessing, not only to ourselves, but to many, many others.

The Lesson

> This is my command: Love each other.
> —John 15:17 NIV

Few people understand what unconditional love is because they have rarely experienced it. Unconditional love is the beginning of real peace and contentment in your heart. It is important to know that God unconditionally loves you. This is difficult to accept because we don't think we deserve it. Deserving has nothing to do with God's loving us. God gave us the gift of life. His gift had nothing to do with deserving. I believe my life was God's gift of love. When we are thankful for this gift no matter what, and realize how precious and priceless it is, we will be kinder and more loving to others as well as to ourselves.

Applying the Lesson

1. Think of a time when you felt really loved. Describe what you think made you feel that way.

_____

_____

_____

_____

2a. Name someone who you believe unconditionally loved you, and/or someone who unconditionally loves you now.

_____

b. Did you also unconditionally love them (i.e., they didn't need to be a certain way for you to love them)?

Yes _____ No _____

c. If not, in what way(s) did you think they should have behaved differently towards you?

_____

_____

_____

_____

_____

_____

_____

_____

_____

3a. In terms of yourself, in what ways do you think you should be different from the way you are, as far as relating to others?

_____

_____

_____

_____

_____

b. Do you get upset with yourself when you don't meet your own expectations?

Yes _____ No _____

c. Do you get upset when others don't meet your expectations?

Yes _____ No _____

4a. Do you think if someone really loves you, they should do what it takes to meet your expectations? (For example, take your good advice and act on it, get organized, etc.)

Yes _____ No _____

b. If you answered "yes," can you see that this is conditional love (putting conditions on what another should do rather than supporting them in being free to be who they are)?

Yes _____ No _____

5a. What criteria do you use for deciding if you love someone or not?

_____

_____

_____

_____

_____

b. Do you realize these criteria are conditions you have put on your relationships?

Yes _____ No _____

c. What do you think about that? _____

_____

_____

_____

6a. What does "unconditional love" mean to you?

_____

_____

_____

_____

b. Have you ever been loved unconditionally?

Yes _____ No _____

How did that feel? _____

_____

_____

c. Have you ever loved someone unconditionally?

Yes _____ No _____

How did that feel? _____

_____

_____

_____

d. Do you agree with the following anonymous quotation?

> "You cannot make someone love you. All you can do is
> be someone who can be loved. The rest is up to them."

Yes _____ No _____

7a. Was there a time when you avoided intimate relationships so
that you wouldn't be disappointed, rejected, or hurt again?

Yes _____ No _____

b. Do you believe God unconditionally loves you?

Yes _____ No _____

c. Would you be willing to ask God to open your heart and give you the faith and strength to allow love in once again?

Yes _____ No _____

d. If not, when would you be willing to do this?

_____

_____

8. The following is one of my favorite poems because it describes love in a very beautiful, poetic way. Although it is entitled, *On Marriage*, it can be applied to any close relationship.

On Marriage
—Kahlil Gibran

Let there be spaces in your togetherness,
And let the winds of heaven dance between you.

Love one another, but make not a bond of love:
Let it rather be a moving sea between the shores of your
   souls.
Fill each other's cup but drink not from one cup.
Give one another of your bread but eat not from the same
   loaf.

Sing and dance together and be joyous, but let each one
    of you be alone,
Even as the strings of a lute are alone though they quiver
    with the same music.

Give your hearts, but not into each other's keeping.
For only the hand of Life can contain your hearts
And stand together yet not too near together:
For the pillars of the temple stand apart,
And the oak tree and the cypress grow not in each other's
    shadow.

Afterthoughts

> If we just take the first steps in the right direction, God
> will support us in the rest of the journey.
> —Norman Vincent Peale
> Author, *The Power of Positive Thinking*

I am sure that those of you who have already begun taking these first steps are on your way towards a life of freedom and a deeper faith in yourself, in God, and in others. The following prayer is one that I wrote when I was needing to make an important decision and wasn't trusting that everything would work out all right. Perhaps it can be a reminder to you that no matter what happens, you are loved and are never alone.

Thank you for taking the time to read these stories. The next step is up to you.

A Sample Daily Prayer

> Lord, I thank you that I can come to you for comfort,
> love, guidance, healing, and clarity about making the
> best decisions for myself.

Help guide me and help bring me a sense of inner peace.

Instill confidence and faith within me that you are in charge, that you are my protector, and that I am not alone.

Thank you again for your love and wisdom.
I will look to you every day to help guide my life.

About the Author

Carol Joy Goldstein-Hall has been a consultant and inspirational speaker since 1984, teaching people the Technologies for Creating® courses containing the principles of the creative process. She was personally trained by Robert Fritz, author of *The Path of Least Resistance, Creating,* and *Your Life as Art.*

Carol is committed to coaching people in living a life of freedom, having the best relationships ever, and organizing their lives around what truly matters to them. She holds a Masters Degree in Education and has an extensive background in language and piano instruction.

In addition, Carol is a member of the National Speaker's Association (NSA) and an inspirational guest speaker for many organizations, churches, conventions, and television programs. Her topics include: *Creating the Life You Choose, Creating your Dream Job,* and *Developing Exquisite Relationships.*

Carol was married to her late husband, Glen Russel Hall, and had a very happy and fulfilling relationship. She also has two children, Nancy and Drew, both of whom have learned to apply the principles of creating to their personal as well as their business lives.

For further information go to *www.technologiesforcreating.com* or contact Carol Joy Goldstein by email at *caroljoyandco@yahoo.com.*

NOTES

NOTES

The man who has heard from God
has the enduring power to engage adversaries,
confront tragedy, and surmount any problem that lies
in his path
because, upon what God has spoken,
he can steadfastly rest.

God is still speaking.
Let us choose the 'good part' of listening obediently to Him.
He has great and mighty things in store for each of us.

> – Dr. Charles Stanley
> Sr. Minister, First Baptist Church
> Atlanta, Georgia
> Author, *How to Listen to God*

Endnotes

[1] Faith as defined in the *American Heritage Dictionary*: a belief that does not rest on logical proof or material evidence; faith in miracles, and a belief and trust in God and in the doctrines expressed in the Scriptures or other sacred works; religious conviction.

[2] In *Medicine Cards, The Discovery of Power through the Ways of Animals*, the authors, Jamie Sams and David Carson, say, "**Porcupine** has many special qualities, and a very powerful medicine: **the power of faith and trust.** The power of faith contains within it the ability to move mountains . . . Trust can open doorways to the creation of space. The space thus created allows others to open their hearts to you and to share their gifts of love, joy, and companionship." The Porcupine is "a gentle reminder not to get caught in the chaos of the adult world where fear, greed and suffering are commonplace."

[3] Dr. Robert Shuller summarized this story as part of a sermon he gave at the Crystal Cathedral.

[4] *Proverbs* is a book of wise sayings, a textbook for teaching people how to live godly lives through the repetition of wise thoughts. Solomon wrote and compiled most of *Proverbs* early in his reign, 965 B.C.

CPSIA information can be obtained at www.ICGtesting.com
Printed in the USA
BVOW031442010213

312182BV00001B/13/P